Great Supreme Court Decisions

BROWN

v.

BOARD
OF EDUCATION

Integrating America's Schools

GREAT SUPREME COURT DECISIONS

Brown v. Board of Education
Dred Scott v. Sandford
Engel v. Vitale
Marbury v. Madison
Miranda v. Arizona
Plessy v. Ferguson
Regents of the University of California v. Bakke
Roe v. Wade

Great Supreme Court Decisions

BROWN
V.
BOARD
OF EDUCATION

Integrating America's Schools

Tim McNeese

CHELSEA HOUSE
PUBLISHERS
An imprint of Infobase Publishing

Brown v. Board of Education

Chelsea House
An imprint of Infobase Publishing
132 West 31st Street
New York, NY 10001

Library of Congress Cataloging-in-Publication Data
McNeese, Tim.
Brown v. Board of Education / Tim McNeese.
    p. cm.—(Great Supreme Court decisions)
  Includes bibliographical references and index.
  ISBN 0-7910-9238-0 (hardcover)
  1. Brown, Oliver, 1918—Trials, litigation, etc.—Juvenile literature. 2. Topeka
(Kan.). Board of Education—Trials, litigation, etc.—Juvenile literature. 3. Seg-
regation in education—Law and legislation—United States—Juvenile literature.
4. African Americans—Civil rights--Juvenile literature. [1. Brown, Oliver, 1918-
—Trials, litigation, etc. 2. Segregation in education—Law and legislation. 3. Af-
rican Americans—Civil rights.] I. Title: Brown versus Board of Education. II.
Title. III. Series.
  KF228.B76M356 2006
  344.73'0798--dc22   2006007324

Series design by Erika K. Arroyo
Cover design by Takeshi Takahashi

Printed in the United States of America

Bang EJB 10 9 8 7 6 5 4 3 2 1

Contents

Introduction

Outside the U.S. Supreme Court building, hundreds of people braving the chilling December weather stood in a line that stretched out away from the stately white marble building. They all waited with hopes of getting a seat in the court's hearing room for what might be, for many of America's blacks, the Supreme Court's most important decision of the century—a century that was barely half complete. The year was 1952. Many arrived at the court building as early as 5:30 that morning. Some spent the night outside the building that had served as the home of the Supreme Court for less than 20 years. The Supreme Court was built at the request of former President William Howard Taft, who, following his presidency was the court's chief justice from 1921 until 1930.

Classical in design, the court building still stands as a towering symbol of order and symmetry. Sixteen marble columns dominate its main entrance, the west portico. The columns hold up the triangular slab of marble pediment. To those who ascend the court building's marble steps to pass through its massive bronze doors, the marble wall presents a sculptured grouping symbolizing Liberty on her throne, surrounded by figures representing Order and Authority. Across the bottom of this scene are chiseled words with a special meaning on this particular day in December: "Equal Justice Under Law."

The court building is a monument to the rule of law in America. An imposing mass of marble, its interior is as impressive as its exterior. Inside, its walls are decorated with symbols of the history of law, from the ancient to the modern world. Many great lawgivers are depicted throughout the halls of the Supreme Court: figures that loomed large on the pages of history, people who delivered frameworks of legal direction, creating codes for human behavior—Moses, Solomon, Confucius, Solon, Muhammad, and Emperor Charlemagne.

As the doors opened, those who had stood outside for hours rushed in, each intent on taking his or her place in the court's hearing room. Three hundred spectators crowded into the room. Soon there were no seats left vacant, and the anxious crowd buzzed with excitement and enthusiasm. In the outer halls, perhaps another 400 filled the corridors, wanting to be a part of American history. Of the hundreds of people who flocked to the Supreme Court building that December morning, about half were black.

Through a side door, nine black-robed men entered the room. As they filed in, each took his place behind a long, dark mahogany bench. They were the court's nine justices, led by Fred Vinson, the court's chief justice. Vinson, "a long-faced man with bushy brows and deep pouches under the eyes,"[1] had only recently been appointed by President Harry Truman to lead the court. Vinson was from Kentucky, and had been in government service for many years. He had served as a congressman from his home state during the years of the Great Depression, had been director of the Office of Economic Stabilization during World War

II, and had been appointed by President Truman as secretary of the treasury. He and Truman had been fellow congressmen years earlier and had become good friends who enjoyed sharing a game of poker. As popular as Vinson was with former President Truman, though, he was not liked by his fellow justices on the court.

As each of the justices took his seat at the bench, they were all aware of the importance of the cases they were to hear that day. The main lawyer who would present his arguments on behalf of several black clients from four different states was certainly no stranger to the court. Thurgood Marshall, a black attorney who had grown up in Maryland, not far from Washington, D.C., had argued before the court on several occasions. He was so well-known for the race cases he had brought before the court during the previous decade that he had become one of the most famous black men in America.

Despite Marshall's reputation for winning Supreme Court cases, however, his opponent that day would be formidable. He was John W. Davis, who was as well-known as Marshall, perhaps more so. At nearly 80 years of age, Davis had already argued 140 cases before the Supreme Court. Decades earlier, when Marshall was attending law school at Howard University, a black school of higher learning, he had sometimes cut classes to sit in on Supreme Court sessions in which Davis was presenting a case. In the courtroom that day in 1952, though, Marshall, dressed in a sharp suit, looked every bit the part of the experienced and successful lawyer. Despite his age, he would present to the nine justices with an unmatched eloquence. There would be moments he would speak with tears in his eyes.

Marshall and his fellow legal colleagues were prepared to present arguments that centered on several race-related cases, and there was much riding on their words. For years, Marshall had worked as a lawyer for the most important civil rights organization in America, the National Association for the Advancement of Colored People (NAACP). Through his tireless efforts, he had won case after case in a long struggle against the nearly universal practice in America that kept the races apart—segregation.

The policy was a matter of law and had been the law of the land stretching back to 1896, when a defiant shoemaker from New Orleans, a mixed-blood Creole named Homer Plessy, had boarded a railcar intended for "whites only" on a train bound north across Louisiana. Plessy took a stand against segregation, but the Supreme Court of the time decided against him, establishing a legal benchmark that ultimately guaranteed white dominance over the nation's black population—"separate but equal." The disappointing decision led to a nearly complete social, political, and cultural division between the races, as whites declared everything from theaters to trains to public drinking fountains and schools off limits to blacks. Blacks would, instead, be provided their own theaters, passenger cars, drinking fountains, and schools, but, in nearly every case, theirs would be second-rate, poor substitutes, designed to remind blacks of their alleged inferiority. As every black person in America knew, the maxim of "separate but equal" was only half supported by whites, generally: Whites wanted everything kept separate; they did not care if things were equal.

Now, 56 years after the *Plessy v. Ferguson* decision, the court was going to sit and listen to Marshall and several other black attorneys present their cases against the concept of "separate but equal." The opening arguments began at 1:05 that afternoon. Marshall was the second attorney to speak that day, and he was the one everyone—justices, reporters, and the assembled crowd as well—was waiting to hear. Even as he approached the bench, "all of the Supreme Court justices came to attention."[2] Marshall began to speak, his booming baritone voice filling the court chamber. There were no microphones, but Marshall did not need one. His ringing words could be heard in every corner, by everyone present. As he spoke that afternoon, Marshall was not speaking for himself, but for those he represented. He spoke for black children in South Carolina who attended school in tar paper shacks. He spoke for black children in Delaware whose

Linda Brown, the 9-year-old girl whose denied entrance to a white elementary school launched the landmark Supreme Court case *Brown v. Board of Education*, is pictured in 1953 in front of the segregated school she attended.

parents had finally decided the schools their children attended were not good enough. He spoke for black students in Prince Edward County, Virginia, who, in protest against their inferior high school, had decided to strike and walk out by the hundreds, until there wasn't a single black student left in Robert R. Moton High.

He also spoke for a young girl named Linda Brown, who lived in Topeka, Kansas, and had completed her first- and second-grade years. Despite living in an integrated neighborhood, where she played with black, Hispanic, and white children alike, young Linda had been forced, by the city's segregation policy, to attend an all-black elementary school seven miles from her home. Because she had to walk part of the way to school, Linda had to leave her house at 7:40 each morning, even though her first class did not begin until 9:00 A.M. She walked two miles every day and passed through a busy and dangerous switchyard of the Rock Island Railway. In the rail yard, Linda sometimes had to dodge great steel locomotives as they steamed past her. Her harrowing walk took her to a street corner where she waited for a bus that took her another five miles to Monroe Elementary School. Sometimes her school bus ran late, and Linda had to wait in rain or snow. Even when the bus arrived on time, Linda would reach the school a half hour early, and the little girl would, again, have to wait outside, sometimes in snow or rain. She had done all this despite living just a few blocks from another school. She had been denied enrollment into that school, though, for it was only open to white students.

A monumental case was unfolding before the nine justices on the Supreme Court. What would be the outcome of the cases waiting to be heard by the highest court in America? What was at stake? Would the legacy of *Plessy v. Ferguson* live on for another 50 years? Would the court hear, really hear, the words of Thurgood Marshall and reconsider the false legacy of "separate but equal"? What would be the future of race relations in America?

EQUAL JUSTICE UNDER LAW

Separating the Races

Throughout U.S. history, the issue of race has never strayed too far out of focus. From the early 1600s, as British subjects established colonies up and down the Atlantic seaboard, blacks were imported from Africa as slaves, to spend their entire lives in the service of their owners. Through the seventeenth and much of the eighteenth centuries, the institution of slavery grew, until hundreds of thousands of black men, women, and children lived, toiled, and struggled under slavery's restrictions. During those decades, slavery became concentrated in the southern colonies—Delaware, Maryland; Virginia, North and South Carolina, and Georgia—where both male and female field hands produced an abundance of tobacco and other crops for their owners.

There were historical moments when serious questions were raised concerning slavery's legitimacy, its morality, and its economics, but the voices of opposition remained few and unassuming. During the Revolutionary War (1775–1783), some patriot leaders suggested that it made little sense for Americans to fight British tyranny to gain their own personal liberty while denying freedom to those of another race. To that end, many of the northern colonies, having become new states, wrote new constitutions that brought slavery to an end within their borders. By the end of the 1700s, slavery had largely become a singularly southern institution.

When profits from tobacco began to decline following the Revolutionary War, a number of observers noted that slavery no longer produced the profits it once had and that the day would soon come when slavery would die a natural death. Then

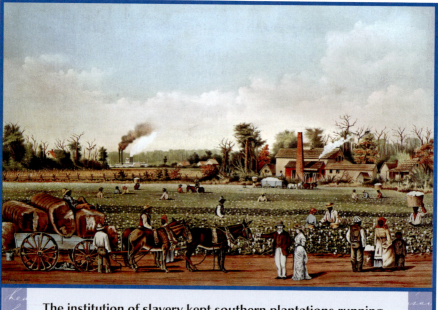

The institution of slavery kept southern plantations running well into the nineteenth century, prolonging the liberation of African Americans for far too long.

came the invention of the cotton gin, a machine that could easily remove the small, sticky green seeds from cotton fiber. Southern agriculture thus turned to cotton cultivation and its high profits. This single invention by northerner Eli Whitney changed the future of slavery, guaranteeing its survival into the nineteenth century and for several more generations.

Throughout the first half of the 1800s, the issue of slavery's expansion into America's western territories remained a constant issue and a flash point between the slave-holding South and northerners who preferred free labor. A new group of anti-slavery advocates, the abolitionists, found their voice. Through endless speeches and a raft of publications, they argued that slavery was an evil, an immorality that tainted everyone involved, both slave and slaveholder alike. In time, the clash over slavery and its future expansion led to violence as abolitionists, such as the fiery John Brown, began to preach, encouraging the destruction of slavery. Using his favorite New Testament scripture, Hebrews 9:22—"without the shedding of blood, there is no forgiveness of sins"—Brown and others campaigned against slavery and even approved murdering its advocates during the struggle over whether the new territory of Kansas would become a slave or a free state.

Brown's campaign ended in 1859 with his execution by the Commonwealth of Virginia, following an attempt on Brown's part to lead a slave rebellion. Nevertheless, the antagonisms between the North and South had reached a fever pitch. Then, in 1860, the candidate for the newly formed Republican Party, an Illinois lawyer named Abraham Lincoln, won the presidential election. Although Lincoln did not believe blacks to be the equals of whites, he opposed the expansion of slavery into the American West. With Lincoln's election, the South believed that slavery and, consequently, their southern way of life, was so significantly threatened that there was nothing they could do but leave the Union and form a separate country of slaveholders. The state of South Carolina seceded, or left, within a month of

Lincoln's election, followed during the next six months by 10 more southern states, from Texas to Virginia.

As Lincoln set himself to the goal of keeping the United States intact, a showdown quickly developed, leading to the U.S. Civil War. The war lasted for four years, from 1861 until 1865. This bloody conflict brought 3 million combatants to a seemingly endless number of battlefields stretching across the country's landscape, and resulted in the deaths of 620,000 men. During this divisive war, President Lincoln made a momentous decision to strike a blow against the South by issuing a presidential edict called the Emancipation Proclamation. This official decree stated that all slaves held on property controlled by the

The Emancipation Proclamation, issued by Abraham Lincoln in 1862, began the federal process of freeing slaves in the United States. The original document is kept in the National Archives in Washington, D.C.

southern Confederacy's government were to be considered free as of January 1, 1863. Although limited in scope, Lincoln's step helped turn the Civil War into a conflict over the ultimate future of slavery in the country.

When the war ended, the South had finally been defeated and the Union ultimately restored. In the aftermath of the conflict, the southern states lay devastated, their cities destroyed, their fields barren, their commercial centers in ruin, and their fundamental labor institution—slavery—at its end. Although Lincoln was assassinated within days of the end of the four-year-long war, Congress, controlled by northerners, began a systematic campaign to completely alter the world of America's 4 million blacks, who had until recently been slaves. Through a series of three amendments to the U.S. Constitution—the Thirteenth, Fourteenth, and Fifteenth—Congress ended the institution of slavery; defined blacks as citizens, thus guaranteeing their rights; and granted voting rights to blacks. The winds of change were blowing for millions of former slaves, and their future appeared brighter than ever.

Through the decade following the Civil War, Congress continued to protect southern blacks through its program of rebuilding the South and redirecting its social and political systems, which became known as Reconstruction. Southern states that had seceded from the Union and fought against the federal government had to be accepted back into the Union, but only after they agreed to protect blacks and their newly gained freedoms. Throughout the remainder of the 1860s and through much of the 1870s, as southern states were reunited with the United States, blacks found new opportunities. Hundreds of black men were elected to various state and national offices. By the 1870s, every legislature of every southern state that had fought for the Confederacy had black legislators. Black mayors were elected, and dozens of black sheriffs were appointed and elected. The days of slavery, for many, began to recede into the fog of time.

While the federal government passed laws and tried to advance the cause of black freedom, though, the majority of white Americans, in both the North and South, were not ready to give up their basic concept of blacks. Most believed that blacks and whites were not truly equal; that blacks were inferior in every conceivable way, physically, psychologically, intellectually, and socially. With this racism deeply instilled into the minds of most whites, blacks remained equal on paper, but translating the intentions of federal law into reality remained a constant uphill battle. Southern states, following their return to the Union, attempted to subvert federal laws guaranteeing the rights of blacks in the South. Although the Fifteenth Amendment had become federal law by 1870, southerners tried to limit black voting. In 1871, the state of Georgia began to require a poll tax as a requisite for voting. Since most blacks were too poor to pay the tax, they were often kept from voting, fulfilling the tax's true purpose. To help ensure that such a tax would not keep any whites from voting, legislators initiated "grandfather clauses." These laws stated that, if a person could not afford to pay the poll tax, he could vote if his grandparents had been able to vote. Therefore, a person could not register to vote if even one of his grandparents had been a slave.

Whites tried to keep blacks down in other, more personal ways. White southerners often worked against blacks by treating them as inferiors and denying them access to social events, as well as public facilities. A white hotel operator might not allow blacks to spend the night in his establishment. Blacks would be kept from doing business in stores and other businesses in the public marketplace. Schools were closed to black students, churches refused black members, and even cemeteries were off limits to blacks.

The United States Congress attempted to right such wrongs by passing a new piece of legislation—the Civil Rights Act of 1875. This act was intended to fill the gaps that existed in guaranteeing black freedoms and rights, despite the Thirteenth,

Fourteenth, and Fifteenth amendments and an earlier act, the Civil Rights Act of 1866. The 1875 act stated that "all persons . . . shall be entitled to the full and equal enjoyment of the accommodations, advantages, facilities, and privileges of inns, public conveyances on land or water, theaters, and other places of public amusement."[3] The act, like all previous acts of Congress that intended to protect the nation's black citizens, had high ideals. In reality, though, the act became law just as the federal government was preparing to end its longstanding program of Reconstruction and control of southern politics. In 1877, Reconstruction officially ended, leaving southern states on their own. With federal oversight eliminated, white

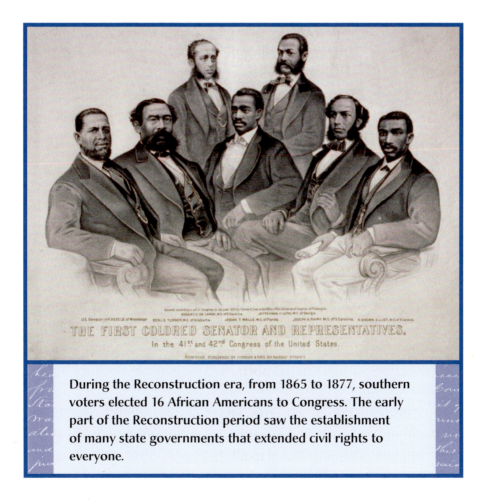

During the Reconstruction era, from 1865 to 1877, southern voters elected 16 African Americans to Congress. The early part of the Reconstruction period saw the establishment of many state governments that extended civil rights to everyone.

southerners began reclaiming control over their state governments. Black legislators were removed from their southern offices, and the new Civil Rights Act of 1875 was mostly ignored. In fact, the act had never really been seriously enforced by the federal government. Six years later, blacks were dealt another serious blow. In 1883, the U.S. Supreme Court declared the Civil Rights Act unconstitutional, claiming it violated the Fourteenth Amendment. Although the amendment protected blacks from discrimination by state governments, the court stated that the law did not limit discrimination practiced by private citizens and businesses. For the nation's hopeful black population, the nation was taking a significant step backward.

THE SPREAD OF SEGREGATION

The federal government had served as the watchdog of newly won black rights across the South following the Civil War, but blacks began to lose their ground during the 1880s and 1890s. Across the South, legislators, other public officials, and even private citizens moved quickly following Reconstruction to halt progress made by blacks during the previous 20 years. In its extremes, whites donned white costumes and hoods as they formed Ku Klux Klan chapters across the South. Founded within a year of the end of the Civil War, the Klan soon became "a terrorist paramilitary force whose main function was to intimidate black citizens who attempted to register to vote or demanded other civil rights."[4] With their identities hidden under their hoods, Klansmen frightened blacks by beating them, burning their homes and belongings, and sometimes by killing anyone, black or white, who tried to help blacks in any way. Since their tactics were typically so extreme, even most southerners did not approve of the Klan.

Intimidating blacks was certainly not limited to the nighttime activities of a group of racist vigilantes such as the Klan. Politicians across the South were also intent on keeping black progress and gains to a minimum. Although national laws guaranteed hundreds of thousands of black citizens the right to vote, white politicians passed state laws designed to keep them from voting. The result was a sharp decline in the number of blacks who voted. The examples tell a sad story. In 1876, after a full decade of Reconstruction, more than 90,000 blacks voted in the presidential election in South Carolina. By the 1888 election, however, South Carolina's black voters numbered only 13,700. The number represented a sharp decline, but some white southerners were still not pleased. In 1895, white politicians in South Carolina changed the state constitution by adding an "understanding clause." Modeled after a similar law created in Mississippi six years earlier, the statute allowed illiterate men to vote if they were able to understand the constitution when a passage was read to them. Using this subjective law, voting officials would generally accept a white voter's understanding but nearly always reject the understanding of a potential black voter.

With such laws, southerners were able to keep blacks from experiencing the true extent of the freedoms they had gained following the Civil War. By the 1890s, all 11 of the southern states that held slaves before the war and joined the Confederacy during the national crisis had passed laws that placed such restrictions on their black citizens:

> These racist laws made blacks feel inferior, because they were denied their basic human rights. Even toilets and drinking fountains were marked "White Only" and "Colored" . . . . It was evident to black citizens that their separate places to eat, sleep, or travel were in much worse shape than those reserved for whites. But the southern whites who had regained power pretended that the separate services for blacks were equal to those of whites.[5]

Across the South, there was an unspoken presumption that blacks were inferior. Whites worked tirelessly to keep the races separated, both through law and custom. Even churches split into separate white and black congregations. As early as the mid-1880s, the South was a world where people lived with walls created by racism. No one understood this separation more than those who were victimized by it. Blacks across the South understood that they were not welcome in the white man's world. Those blacks who attempted to cross the line were typically greeted with hostility and reprisals. Blacks learned to steer clear of white businesses and social scenes. An 1885 issue of a Tennessee newspaper editorial noted this dual world: "The colored people make no effort to obtrude themselves upon the whites in the public schools, their churches, their fairs, their Sunday-schools, their picnics, their social parties, hotels or banquets."[6]

THE CONCEPT OF "SEPARATE BUT EQUAL"

Segregation spread into additional corners of the South during the 1880s, with the creation of laws restricting black access to public transportation. This segregation created a severe problem for blacks. It was one thing for a black person to be denied a hotel room by a racist innkeeper. There were, perhaps, other accommodations available. But when states denied access to public transportation systems, such as railroads and streetcars, the alternatives for blacks were often reduced to zero. The first segregation law intended to restrict black access to railroads was passed in Tennessee in 1881, just four years after the end of Reconstruction. A similar law was passed in Florida in 1887. These laws allowed railroads to provide separate accommodations for black and white rail passengers. The railroads affected did not like such laws, since they required the railroads to provide additional cars on their trains, even on lines that did not attract significant numbers of black passengers. The "black only" cars were generally second class in quality.

The law created in Tennessee in 1881 was different from these earlier attempts to limit black access to first-class railroad passenger cars. In an attempt to abide by the letter of the laws created to protect blacks during Reconstruction, Tennessee's law was built on the concept of "separate but equal." The goal of

EARLIER "SEPARATE CAR LAWS"

As southerners became intent on keeping the black and white races apart in as many aspects of public life as possible, they created laws intended to do just that. By the 1880s, states such as Tennessee and Mississippi, passed laws that required blacks and whites to occupy different railroad cars.

These laws were not the first attempt to limit what rail cars could be used by blacks. Similar laws had been passed in earlier decades, but these laws were significantly different. (The first "separate car law" was established as early as 1841, not in a southern state, but in Massachusetts.) Following the Civil War, however, southern states created many such laws. In 1865, Mississippi legislators passed a law prohibiting "any freedman, Negro, or mulatto, to ride in any first class passenger cars, set apart, or used by and for white persons."*

The Mississippi law did not completely separate the races from one another on railroad cars, though. The law presumed that blacks would ride alongside whites in "second-class" cars— those on which smoking took place and whose occupants were often a poorer and rougher crowd. Then in 1868, the Texas legislature passed yet another "Jim Crow" law for railroad passengers. This time, the law established completely separate cars for both blacks and whites. The law applied only to railroads operating within the state of Texas.

Such early separate car laws did not remain in effect. When Texas, Mississippi, and all the other states of the defeated Confederacy fell under the control of the federal government during Reconstruction, these early separate car laws were removed from the books.

*Quoted in C. Vann Woodward, *The Strange Career of Jim Crow*. New York: Oxford University Press, 1957, p. xiii.

the law was the same: To keep the races separated on public transportation without an appearance of violating federal laws guaranteeing blacks rights. "Separate but equal" was a concept that gave nearly everyone—blacks and whites alike—a system that was not, at least on the surface, blatantly racist in nature. Blacks and whites would be able to ride on the same railroads but would not have direct contact with one another. Whites would ride in their rail cars, and blacks would enjoy their own cars. As long as the two car types were roughly equivalent in quality and comfort—"separate but equal"—the law was satisfied and so was everyone else.

Other states saw the merit of such a concept in determining railroad ridership. Southern states soon created similar laws. Florida followed suit, then Mississippi, Texas, and North Carolina. Although these laws were generally alike, there were variations. Florida's had the appearance of being more noble than Tennessee's law, in stating that "no white person shall be permitted to ride in a Negro car or to insult or annoy Negroes in such car."[7] Initially, these new "separate but equal" laws were widely accepted by both blacks and whites. Blacks welcomed the promise of "separate but equal" railroad accommodations, but it did not take long to see the actual intent of these laws. The railroad regulations were devised as a smoke screen to hide the preference on the part of whites to keep blacks separated from them, because they perceived blacks to be inferior. In addition, "separate but equal" rarely ever materialized. The cars provided for black passengers on southern railroads were typically less than equal to those provided for whites. The only part of "separate but equal" that whites generally wanted was the part that provided separation.

THE LOUISIANA SEPARATE CAR LAW

Such laws spread across the South during the final years of the nineteenth century. A separate car law was passed in Louisiana in 1890, even as the state's 18 black legislators refused to

[From the Independent Monitor, Tuscaloosa, Alabama, September 1, 1868.]
A PROSPECTIVE SCENE IN THE CITY OF OAKS, 4TH OF MARCH, 1869.

" Hang, curs, hang !   *   Their complexion is perfect gallows.   Stand fast, good
fate, to their hanging !   *   *   *   *   *   *   *   *   If they be not born to be hanged, our case is miserable.''
    The above cut represents the fate in store for those great pests of Southern society—
the carpet-bagger and scalawag—if found in Dixie's land after the break of day on the
4th of March next.

This cartoon, which was published in an Alabama newspaper in 1868, warned that the Ku Klux Klan would get to carpetbaggers and scalawags if they stayed in the South.

support it. This law established segregation on trains running within the state, requiring railroads to provide "separate but equal accommodations for the white and colored races."[8] Even if a black passenger had the money to buy a first-class ticket to ride in the best passenger car, he or she would not be allowed and would have to ride in the second-class car instead. The law was met with a furor of protest in New Orleans, where the city's blacks, whites, and Creoles (those of mixed race) regularly mingled in social settings. A local group, the American Citizens' Equal Rights Association of Louisiana (ACERA), soon set out to challenge the law. They hoped to take the law to court, where a judge or judges might declare it unconstitutional. Between the ACERA and its offshoot organization, the Citizens' Committee, which was established formally in

September 1891, these organizations led opposition to the Separate Car Act of 1890.

As the ACERA, and, more specifically, the Citizens' Committee, set its sights on Louisiana's Separate Car Act, the members decided to "demonstrate its absurdity by enlisting the support of a black man who was almost indistinguishable from a white person."[9] Homer Plessy was a lifelong resident of New Orleans, a young, mixed-race Creole who was one-eighth black. He was so light-skinned that he could pass for white. In fact, he had done so several times on the state's railroads, buying "first-class" tickets and sitting in the "whites only" car. In the summer of 1892, Plessy bought a "first-class" ticket on the East Louisiana Railroad. His light skin did not give away the fact that, by Louisiana law, Homer Plessy was considered a black man. Only after the train got underway did he officially inform the train's conductor that he was not actually white. Plessy was subsequently arrested, booked in the local precinct house, and almost immediately bailed out of jail by a member of the Citizens' Committee, all according to plan.

During the next four years, Homer Plessy's case went its course through the American legal system, until it landed on the docket of the U.S. Supreme Court. Plessy's lawyers argued that the separate car law was unconstitutional, claiming it violated the Thirteenth and Fourteenth amendments, federal laws that guaranteed the rights and privileges of the nation's blacks. The court did not prove friendly to Plessy's case. On May 18, 1896, the Supreme Court, by a margin of 7 to 1, decided to uphold the constitutionality of the Louisiana Separate Car Law and the validity of the concept of "separate but equal."

The court's decision set an ominous tone for the future of black rights and progress for decades to come. Immediately, such laws would be passed by states throughout the South. By 1892, eight southern states, including Louisiana, had established separate car laws. Following the *Plessy v. Ferguson* decision, other states adding their own restrictive laws included

South Carolina (1898), North Carolina (1899), Virginia (1900), Maryland (1904), and Oklahoma (1907). The number of "Jim Crow" laws expanded dramatically as southern legislators created new ways to restrict the freedoms of the country's blacks. ("Jim Crow" refers to laws that were designed to treat blacks as inferiors. Usually state laws passed after the Civil War through World War II, these laws typically discriminated against blacks by denying them their equal rights.)

At every turn, blacks found their progress stifled and their rights diminished. Eight million men, women, and children of color were impacted by the short-sightedness of the *Plessy v. Ferguson* decision. Millions of others would, throughout the first half of the twentieth century, be similarly affected. The reason is thus: This single court case, with it's support of the misleading concept of "separate but equal," would remain the law of the land for the next 56 years.

EQUAL·JUSTICE·UNDER·LAW·

2

Separate, but Equal

ith the Supreme Court decision *Plessy v. Ferguson*, Jim Crow became the standard for southern laws pertaining to blacks. It had been the decision of the court's majority that "separate but equal" was valid and legal. The court had stated that Louisiana's Separate Car Act was not a violation of the U.S. Constitution's Fourteenth Amendment, explaining that the amendment "only guaranteed the political equality of Negroes, not their social equality."[10] Everything from lunch counters to libraries, parks to public accommodations, and drinking fountains to toilets were separated by law, always under the false expectation of "separate but equal." In their never-ending quest to keep blacks in a state of legal inferiority, whites left no stone unturned:

> [Blacks] had to use separate hospitals when they were ill, and, after they died, find their final rest in black cemeteries. Florida and North Carolina prohibited white children from using textbooks that had been touched by blacks. Alabama even made it a crime for blacks and whites to play checkers together. In Mississippi, blacks and whites had to use separate phone booths. Any Negro who inadvertently crossed the color line could expect to be severely punished.[11]

Although none of this legal discrimination could be considered acceptable by blacks, the impact of such laws on black children was especially disgraceful. When the Supreme Court decided to uphold the concept of "separate but equal" in its

Plessy v. Ferguson decided that blacks should have "separate but equal" facilities. It was simple enough to find drinking fountains and restrooms of equal standard, but receiving an education equal to that granted to whites proved much more of a challenge.

decision regarding *Plessy v. Ferguson*, the justices went further than simply justifying segregation on public transportation. The court also stated its acceptance of segregation in the public schools in the nation's capital, Washington, D.C. The court included this point because, technically, these schools had been established and administered by the U.S. Congress, which makes the laws for the District of Columbia. Because Congress had sanctioned segregation in these schools, the court argued, state laws that similarly discriminated should not be challenged, either.

EARLIER GAINS IN EDUCATION

Following the *Plessy v. Ferguson* decision, schools would be redirected toward the artificial standard of "separate but equal." Despite this, there had been bright signs concerning blacks and opportunities for them to receive a public education in earlier decades. It was uncommon for tax dollars to pay for black schools until after the Civil War. Following the war, however, a new emphasis was placed on the value of education for America's youth, whether black or white. The nation was changed; it had, in fact, been changed by the war itself. The country was moving slowly away from an almost entirely agriculturally-based economy to one that depended on manufacturing. The business of America during the decades following the Civil War was business. Children needed to learn to read and write, and they needed additional academic skills, as well, to find their place in the new, modern world that was spinning toward the twentieth century.

Public schools across the North were typically ahead of those in the South, where states spent comparatively less public money on education. During the 1870s, however, education in the South became a new priority. As the number and quality of southern schools expanded, though, they were often not open to black students. Instead, the job of educating the South's blacks (many of whom only recently had been slaves or were the children of slaves) was picked up by the Freedmen's Bureau, created by Congress in 1865. The bureau was designed to help blacks transition from slavery to freedom by providing food, housing, medical care, and limited education (to teach them how to read and write). The task proved daunting. The vast majority of former slaves were illiterate, and there were not enough schools available. Through the Freedman's Bureau, more than 4,000 basic schools were established across the South, but these were only able to reach about one out of every four school-aged children of former slaves. Still, it was progress.

- The Freedmen's Bureau, however, was funded only until 1872. Then, the federal government packed up and abandoned the majority of the schools it had established across the South. Even when the Freedman's Bureau stopped administering these needed educational systems, though, many of their schools were kept open, financed by funds provided through state and local taxes. The move was just another opportunity for southern states to keep blacks separated from whites. Some southern states even passed specific segregation laws directed at schools. (Segregated schools could also be found in other parts of the United States at this time, but they were less common than in the South. All told, half of the 50 states have had segregation laws on their books at any given time, in an attempt to keep black and white students apart.)

By the 1890s, segregated schools were the norm in the United States. The segregation that existed did not guarantee equality, of course. White schools were typically better than black schools—the facilities were better, and there were more books and more opportunities. Black schools were often little more than run-down shacks, often without running water or electricity. There were usually no books. The teachers were poorly paid and often undereducated themselves. One black woman, Septima Clark, remembered her days teaching in a rural South Carolina school on Johns Island in the early 1900s:

Here I was, a high-school graduate, eighteen years old, principal in a two-teacher school with 132 pupils ranging from beginners to eighth graders, with no teaching experience, a schoolhouse constructed of boards running up and down, with no slats on the cracks, and a fireplace at one end of the room that cooked the pupils immediately in front of it but allowed those in the rear to shiver and freeze on their uncomfortable, hard, back-breaking benches.[12]

Even with the arrival of the twentieth century, the southern states typically underfunded black schools and at times appeared to completely disregard them. Prior to World War I, the South had almost no public high schools for black students. The problem was not exclusively a rural one. As late as 1915, of each of the 23 southern cities with a population greater than 20,000 each—a list that included New Orleans, Charleston, and Charlotte—none of them had a black high school. By comparison, these cities boasted 36 high schools combined, all intended for white students only.

Sometimes blacks chose to protest these conditions and slights, and took their cases to court. Just a year after the 1896 *Plessy v. Ferguson* decision, blacks decided to sue school officials in Augusta, Georgia, when the city's only black secondary school, War High School, was turned into a black primary school. The case reached the U.S. Supreme Court in 1899, and the court's decision in *Cumming v. Richmond County [Georgia] Board of Education* would be unanimous. The court decided against the city's blacks, refusing to accept the claim made by lawyers representing Augusta's black children that closing the only black high school was a violation of the concept of "separate but equal," which the court had upheld in earlier decisions. Ironically, the court had somehow ignored the fact that Augusta had two white high schools, one for boys and one for girls, but no high school for black students.

With such a lack of secondary schools available to black students, many of those who wanted to continue their education past the primary grades were forced to attend a black college or university that might offer a high-school certificate. Such programs were not rare, since black colleges and universities recognized the lack of available high schools across the South. One example can be seen in the circumstances of a young black student from South Carolina. In 1911, Benjamin Mays, then 16 years old, left his home, took passage on a train with separate cars for blacks and whites, and traveled 100 miles to South Carolina State College, where he enrolled in the seventh grade. Five years later, he graduated with his high-school diploma, then graduated four years later from Bates College in Maine.

A common thread running through southern schools was the constant indignities and inequities placed on black children. A Department of Education Annual Report for the state of South Carolina for the 1908–1909 school year tells a typical story. The state had 2,354 schools for black students and 2,712 for whites, even though the number of black students (181,000) was greater than the number of white students (154,000). In the black schools, the student-to-teacher ratio was 63 to 1. In the white schools, the ratio was 35 to 1. Blacks schools averaged only 15 weeks of school a year, whereas white schools averaged 25. There were wide gaps between teacher salaries, as well. The real tragedy, however, lay in other telling numbers. The total expenditures provided for the white schools of South Carolina amounted to nearly $1.6 million, although the monies allotted by the state for its black schools was just over $300,000. Despite the concept of "separate but equal," black and white schools across the South were anything but equal. Circumstances did not improve during the following years; they only became worse. In 1910, for example, across the 11 former-Confederate states of the South, the average spent on educating a white child was $9.45 (about $194 today), whereas the amount spent on a black child, if a school was even available, was only $2.90 (about $59 today).

Such circumstances led many blacks to make the decision to leave the South altogether. Between 1910 and 1930, a regional shift took place in America, one referred to by modern historians as "The Great Migration." During those two decades, more than one million blacks left the South for northern destinations, most choosing to move to various urban centers—St. Louis, Cincinnati, Cleveland, Detroit, New York City, and Philadelphia. There was discrimination in the North, as well, but blacks could enjoy a greater level of acceptance, state and local laws were less restrictive toward them, and opportunities were greater. This number of blacks migrating to the North was still only a small fraction of the total black population of the South by the 1920s. Nine million remained in the South, and many of them—about three of every four—lived in rural poverty, often working as sharecroppers, on land that belonged to whites. They were unable to advance, generally, in society. They were kept down by hundreds of segregationist and race-based laws and were even subject to violence.

These decades, then, the 1920s and 1930s, falling between the two world wars, were a time that brought little progress concerning black schools and the advancement of black public education. With each passing year, the gap between the best white schools and the worst black schools was widening at an alarming rate. Schools were becoming more advanced, too, with increasingly difficult and varied curriculums that went far beyond earlier days, when schools were typically one-room buildings where a teacher or two taught reading, writing, some arithmetic, and, on occasion, a civics lesson. Among America's blacks, though, there were leaders who saw the importance of the children of their race receiving a quality education.

BLACK LEADERS AND NEW DIRECTIONS

One early black leader who emphasized education was Booker T. Washington. Washington had been born into slavery in western Virginia. Having fortunately received a basic education and driven by his personal ambition, he attended the Hampton Institute, which taught industrial, domestic, and agricultural

classes. Soon after his graduation in 1881, Washington was offered the opportunity to found a similar college in Alabama:
the Tuskegee Institute. He had emerged from Hampton convinced that blacks needed education, and at Tuskegee he encouraged the study of agriculture and industry. Washington's
Tuskegee soon became a model education system, designed to
teach blacks how to be good farmers, craftsmen, shopkeepers,
and domestic servants. His model would not go unchallenged.

By the turn of the century, Washington was being criticized
by another educated black leader, W.E.B. DuBois, a graduate of
Fisk College and a Harvard-trained scholar. DuBois was critical
of Washington's seemingly limited agenda for black education.
He believed blacks should be just as educated as whites, that they
should study the same academic curriculum. He thought Washington's Tuskegee model of education only turned blacks into
better examples of the kinds of workers whites wanted them to

Scholar, civil rights activist, and NAACP co-founder W.E.B. DuBois agreed with Booker T. Washington's view that African Americans should receive a quality education. DuBois, however, argued that blacks should pursue full educations in their own right, rather than improving their vocational skills as Washington suggested.

be. DuBois wanted blacks to pursue other roles for themselves, and education would be the key:

> If my own city of Atlanta had offered it today, the choice between 500 Negro college graduates—forceful, busy, ambitious men of property and self-respect—and 500 black cringing vagrants and criminals, the popular vote in favor of the criminals would be simply overwhelming. Why? Because they want Negro crime? No, not that they fear Negro crime less, but that they fear Negro ambition and success more. They can deal with crime by chain-gang and lynch law, or at least they think they can, but the South can conceive neither machinery nor place for the educated, self-reliant, self-assertive black man.[13]

For DuBois, black education had to be steered away from Washington's Tuskegee model. DuBois also believed that blacks needed to change tactics: They needed to steer away from Washington's general inclination to avoid confrontation or make waves that might cause whites to turn against blacks. Washington told "colored men to be patient" and to keep clear of anything that smacked of agitation. But DuBois believed that segregation across the South would only be ended by blacks demanding justice and equality. DuBois wrote of his desire to move beyond the slow approach to change that Washington embodied to so many blacks:

> So far as Mr. Washington preaches Thrift, Patience, and Industrial Training for the masses, we must hold up his hands and strive with him. . . . But so far as Mr. Washington apologizes for injustice, North or South . . . and opposes higher training and ambition of our brighter minds—so far as he, the South, or the Nation, does this—we must unceasingly and firmly oppose them.[14]

DuBois, the first black American to receive a doctorate from Harvard University, wanted change and change immediately.

He wanted to see the black vote restored, and he hung much of his hope for the future of America's blacks on education.

Other black leaders, as well as some whites, agreed with DuBois. In the spring of 1909, a group of 300 black and white leaders, including social workers, writers, educators, journalists, and other professionals, came together in New York City for a national conference to discuss the issues blacks faced across the United States and to search for the appropriate solutions. DuBois was a keynote speaker at this convention, speaking of the "new slavery" that blacks lived under in America, one based on oppression that included voting restrictionns, limited educational opportunities, and the flat-out denial of many of their civil rights.

When the group met the following year, they created a new name for their organization: the National Association for the Advancement of Colored People (NAACP). It was destined to become the most important American civil rights organization of the twentieth century. Perhaps ironically, in those early days of the NAACP, the organization's leadership was generally white. DuBois was the group's only black officer, serving as director of publicity and research.

To spread the word of the group's goals and intentions, the NAACP published a monthly journal, *The Crisis*. Its first issue was published in November 1910, with a printing of 1,000 copies. By 1913, the magazine had 30,000 regular subscribers, the vast majority of whom were not even NAACP members. (The organization had a membership that year of about 3,000.)

By the end of its first decade in print, the publication's monthly print run reached 100,000. For more than a quarter century, *The Crisis* was the most important publication in support of the advancement of black rights. Through its pages, DuBois and others pounded out their drumbeat in favor of blacks standing up for themselves and challenging the status quo: "Agitate, then, brother; protest, reveal the truth and refuse to be silenced .... A moment's let up, moment's acquiescence, means

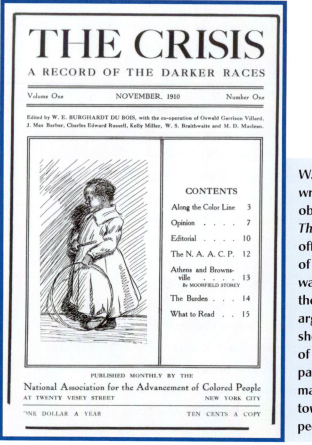

W.E.B. DuBois wrote that the objective of *The Crisis*, the official magazine of the NAACP, was to "set forth those facts and arguments which show the danger of race prejudice, particularly as manifested today toward colored people."

a chance for the wolves of prejudice to get at our necks."[15] These words would become an inspiring call for blacks throughout the twentieth century.

THE NAACP GOES TO COURT

Speaking for blacks across the country, the NAACP grew rapidly, forming 50 branch chapters within its first five years. The organization had lawyers at its disposal, legal experts who filed suits intended to knock Jim Crow laws out of existence. In 1914, the NAACP experienced one of its first legal victories when it succeeded in taking Oklahoma's "grandfather clause" to the U.S. Supreme Court and getting it overturned in a decision cited as

Guinn v. United States. Three years later, the NAACP won yet another case, this one addressing housing restrictions against blacks. This 1917 decision—*Buchanan v. Warley*—struck down a law in Louisville, Kentucky, that had kept blacks from living in neighborhoods where the majority population was white.

These cases were crucial wins for the NAACP, because, typically, court cases that had earlier challenged Jim Crow laws had not been successful. After the Supreme Court's decision in *Plessy v. Ferguson* (1896), various groups with both black and white members filed suits to challenge circumstances that they considered "separate but unequal." The 1899 case *Cumming v. Richmond County Board of Education* had been such a situation. The case challenged the closing of the only black high school in Richmond County, Georgia. Supreme Court justices, however, decided in favor of the white-dominated school board. In an ironic twist, the very justice who had been the lone dissenter in the *Plessy v. Ferguson* decision, Justice John Marshall Harlan, wrote the majority decision this time, against the black parents who had filed the suit in opposition to the school board's decision and in support of their own children.

Harlan wrote in his decision that it was not the role of the federal government to interfere in local school board decisions. Although he agreed that "the benefits and burdens of public taxation must be shared by citizens without discrimination against any class on account of race," he insisted that "the education of people in schools maintained by state taxation is a matter belonging to the respective states, and any interference on the part of Federal authority with the management of such schools cannot be justified."[16] Although Harlan was sympathetic to the plight of blacks denied their education by a local school board, his strong support of state's rights kept him and the court's majority from deciding against a local school board.

Although this Supreme Court decision was a disappointment to blacks across the country, another Supreme Court decision less than 10 years later was even more disappointing. The case was *Berea College v. Kentucky*. Berea College's origins dated back to 1859, when it was founded as an unsegregated Southern college. Following the *Plessy v. Ferguson* decision, however, Kentucky passed a statute that required all unsegregated educational institutions within the state to attend to hold segregated classes, resulting in a first-time separation of the races at Berea. Not only that, but classes for whites and blacks had to be held at sites at least 25 miles from one another. Berea College did not intend to abide by this new Kentucky law. The college, after all, did not receive state support through taxes and did not believe it had to respond to the new state law. Since the college had been founded as a religious school, the Kentucky

LEGAL LOSSES FOR OTHER RACES

Two important Supreme Court decisions—*Cumming v. Richmond County Board of Education* and *Berea College v. Kentucky*—were legal losses before the founding of the NAACP, but there would be legal losses that followed the institution's establishment, as well. In 1927, yet another Supreme Court ruling appeared to provide another foundation stone for segregated schools to rest on. The case rose out of Bolivar County, Mississippi, where the father of a young Chinese-American girl, nine-year-old Martha Lum, tried to enroll her in a white school. (He knew how inferior the local blacks schools were and wanted his daughter to attend a better school.) Local school officials refused to admit Martha Lum to a white school. The Lums then took their case to court. When a Mississippi court decided against Lum, the case was appealed to the U.S. Supreme Court.

Mr. Lum did not intend to question the constitutionality of segregated schools or the concept of "separate but equal" in this case.

law "denied the free practice of religion, a right guaranteed by the First Amendment to the Constitution."[17]

Despite the logic of Berea College's situation, the Kentucky Supreme Court decided against the college, although it did seriously question the 25-mile separation restriction. Unprepared to abide by the state's high-court decision, college officials and lawyers appealed their case to the U.S. Supreme Court, which upheld the decision of the Kentucky court. The justices argued that, when Berea College had been founded, it had received a charter from the state of Kentucky. This meant, the court decided, that Berea College was bound to abide by the laws of the state. In addition, the court did not agree that segregated classes would significantly violate the college's mission as a religious

He simply wanted his daughter to attend a good school. The court's majority, in a decision cited as *Gong Lum v. Rice*, decided to deny Lum's request. They cited *Cumming v. Richmond County* as their precedent, stating that the "right and power of the state to regulate the method of providing for the education of its youth at public expense is clear."* It was not the place of the federal government to interfere in the segregationist policies of public schools in any state. These words were written by the Supreme Court's chief justice, former president William Howard Taft. The cumulative impact of such cases, including the Cumming decision and the Berea College decision, made one thing clear about the future of American education: It was going to remain segregated for a long time into an otherwise uncertain future.

* Quoted in James Tackach, *Brown v. Board of Education*. San Diego: Lucent Books, 1998, p. 31.

school to "promote the cause of Christ."[18] The decision would mark a sad day for the nation's blacks and for the college. The court had stated, basically, that segregation could be placed on any educational institution in the country, even if its officials, constituencies, and students did not support it. Nearly 50 years of tradition at Berea College soon came to an end, as its classes were segregated for the first time.

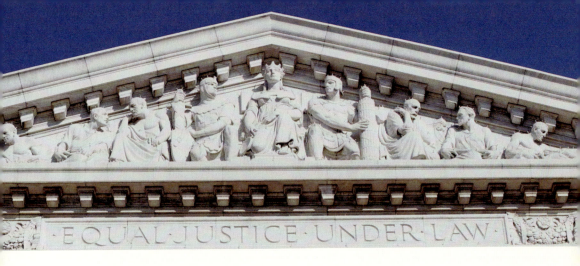

EQUAL·JUSTICE·UNDER·LAW·

New Cases
and the NAACP

Although cases such as *Berea College v. Kentucky, Cumming v. Richmond County,* and *Gong Lum v. Rice* were considered setbacks for the cause of bringing down segregation in America, the NAACP remained dedicated to its campaign of challenging "Jim Crow" laws in court. During the 1930s, the civil rights organization was prepared to take on other cases.

In May, 1933, just weeks following the inauguration of Franklin Roosevelt as president of the United States, the NAACP gained a new chief attorney. He was Charles Houston, who was then serving as the dean of the Howard University Law School. (Howard University was founded after the Civil War and today

The NAACP held its national conference in Atlanta, Georgia, in 1920. The organization is still influential, nearly 100 years after its inception.

is still an important academic institution for black university students.) Houston was just the man for the job of directing the legal wing of the NAACP, since he was an expert in civil rights law.

Houston was also one of the most brilliant legal minds in America. A native of Washington, D.C., Houston had graduated from Amherst College in 1915 when he was only 19 years old. After teaching English for a short time at Howard University, he and other young black men joined the NAACP and immediately lobbied Congress to create a program to train black military officers. Shortly afterward, the United States entered World War I. After he completed training at the black officers' training facility he helped established in Des Moines, Iowa, Houston was commissioned as a first lieutenant. He entered the war in France, where he served in a segregated black unit, the 92nd Division. Houston and some of his fellow black soldiers sometimes fell against the hard edge of racism delivered by their fellow (white) soldiers. In one unfortunate incident,

Houston was almost lynched by a gang of out-of-control white troops. He emerged from his wartime service having been deeply impacted by such racism and vowed he would spend his professional career fighting such attitudes: "The hate and scorn showered on us Negro officers by our fellow Americans convinced me that there was no sense in my dying for a world ruled by them. I made up my mind that if I got through this war I would study law and use my time fighting for men who could not strike back."[19]

After his return stateside, Houston entered Harvard Law School in the autumn of 1919. His academic record at Harvard was brilliant and exemplary. He became the first black law student to serve as editor of the *Harvard Law Review*. It was during his days at Harvard that Houston was first noticed by two Harvard law professors, Roscoe Pound and Felix Frankfurter. Pound was an early advocate of "sociological jurisprudence," a concept that encouraged judges to render decisions after determining the social and economic impact that would result. As for Frankfurter, he took Houston under his wing, and turned him into the lawyer he would become. Frankfurter and Houston would cross paths decades later over the *Brown* case.

The brilliant Houston graduated in the top 5 percent of his class. By 1922, he received his initial law degree, the L.L.B.; then, the following year, took his S.J.D., the highest law degree offered in the United States. He went on immediately to further study, taking classes on the civil law system in Spain, at the University of Madrid. Following this study, he returned to Washington, D.C., where he went into legal practice with his father, William LePre Houston, who had graduated with a law degree from Howard University in 1892. Over the next few years, young Houston practiced law and worked as a part-time instructor at Howard University, teaching law classes. By 1929, he had become an associate law professor and vice dean of Howard Law School. He soon made his mark on the law school as one of its most important administrators.

Although Howard's law school was more than 60 years old, it had struggled throughout the latter decades of the nineteenth century with small numbers of students. Even as Houston took his post as vice dean, the law school was set up with many of the law instructors as part-time academics, teaching their courses at night, after days spent at their regular jobs, working in government offices or at various legal practices. Although this was a common practice at law schools in

It was the idea of Charles Houston (1895–1950) to argue that education in the United States for blacks and whites was separate but certainly not equal, and therefore not complying with the *Plessy v. Ferguson* decision.

and around Washington and other cities, it had not proven very successful at Howard. The school was not even accredited by the American Bar Association (ABA) or the newly formed Association of American Law Schools (AALS). (At that time, the ABA did not even accept black lawyers into its ranks.) In addition, Houston was not happy with the curriculum offered at Howard Law School. He decided to make some changes.

Houston was a product of the Harvard Law School system, which was decidedly different in structure and emphasis than Howard. The Harvard system put its emphasis on having full-time students who would be focused on nothing but their law studies. Harvard "stressed that law should be the province of full-time students led through the rigors of legal analysis under the tutelage of full-time legal academics."[20] Using the Harvard model as his guide, Houston set out to completely revamp Howard's system:

> He eliminated the night program. He eased out many part-time professors, cut the size of the student body, and imposed a demanding rigor in the teaching of Howard's young lawyers-in-training. Houston's improvements were noted with approval by the larger legal community. In 1931 both the AALS and the ABA formally accredited the Howard Law School.[21]

In addition to these changes to Howard's system, Houston gave the school's legal curriculum a new emphasis: He believed that black schools such as Howard should emphasize civil rights law. To that end, he created the first civil rights law course taught at any law school in America. He beefed up the school's library, making it one of the best repositories of legal materials and files on civil rights precedents in the country. Other law schools began to look at Howard as the magnet law school for the nationwide struggle against injustice, segregation, and "Jim Crow." From his unique position at Howard, Houston was able to serve both the law school and the NAACP.

Through the 1930s, Houston helped oversee cases sponsored by the NAACP that resulted in singular successes, especially in helping establish equal pay for black teachers. He won a similar case in Virginia, one cited as *Alston v. School Board of City of Norfolk* (1940).

Next, Houston decided to target segregation in universities and colleges, particularly in graduate and professional schools. He knew that segregation in these more advanced academic institutions was as commonplace as it was in elementary and secondary schools. Also, Houston knew that such cases had great potential to bring about maximum change. Since there were fewer graduate schools than public schools, each case could cause greater ripples of change. One of the first successful cases for the NAACP in this legal arena was a 1936 decision, *Pearson v. Murray*. Donald Murray was a graduate of Amherst College, just as Houston was, and he applied to attend the law school at the University of Maryland. Although his student record was exemplary, he was rejected. The dean of the Maryland school informed Murray that his school did not accept black law students, and he suggested that Murray might want to apply to Howard University instead. The Maryland dean even offered scholarship monies provided by the state of Maryland to pay for Murray's education. A case soon followed, filed by lawyers for the NAACP.

At issue was the University of Maryland's policy of providing state monies to provide an education for black students outside of the state and whether or not that policy abided by the legal concept of "separate but equal." The state provided $10,000 for scholarships to be divided potentially between 50 black students at a rate of $200 each. (In addition to being an inadequate amount of funding, the state legislature had only created the fund following the filing of the Murray suit by the NAACP.) The courts in Maryland decided in Murray's favor. Both a trial judge and the Maryland Court of Appeals decided against the university's policy. Murray had been denied "admis-

Thurgood Marshall, Charles Houston, and Donald Gaines Murray are pictured in 1935, preparing Murray's desegregation case against the University of Maryland.

sion [to the University of Maryland] on the sole ground of his color."[22] Accepting white students into the Maryland university system and denying blacks did not abide by the *Plessy v. Ferguson* decision of "separate but equal." The decision constituted a win for the NAACP's campaign against segregation. Although the decision only applied directly to Maryland, it could serve as a precedent and inspiration for other states to change their laws. The case was singularly important for an additional reason: The young attorney who had presented the case alongside Houston was a black lawyer he had hired—Thurgood Marshall—who would one day play an important role in the *Brown* case of the early 1950s. (Houston had hired Marshall on as an NAACP attorney late in 1933 and assigned him an office in Baltimore. By

1936, he had moved Marshall to the civil rights organization's headquarters on Fifth Avenue in New York City.) In assisting Houston in this case, Marshall likely emerged with a sense of personal satisfaction and even vindication. Marshall was from Maryland and had attempted to enter the University of Maryland law school in 1930 but had been denied.

One of the most important cases Houston and his colleagues took on for the NAACP would involve a young black student from Missouri, Lloyd Gaines. Gaines was among the best of his class at Lincoln University and the senior president. Lincoln was a black university established by the state of Missouri. At graduation, Gaines wanted to attend the University of Missouri School of Law, but the state institution, just as was the case with the University of Maryland, did not admit black students. The case situations were significantly different, however. Under the laws of Missouri, Lincoln University had the authority to establish its own law school but had not done so because of a lack of demand. In that case, Gaines was directed to another Missouri law, Section 9622 of the 1929 Revised Statutes of Missouri. This law required the state to pay tuition for black students from Missouri who might enroll in the law schools of neighboring states. In this manner, the state of Missouri was attempting to live under the expectations of "separate but equal."

As with the Murray-Maryland case, one of the main issues was whether the amount of money provided by the state of Missouri for blacks to attend out-of-state law schools was adequate, compared to the amount provided for white students. In 1937, the Missouri Supreme Court decided against Gaines in the case of *State ex rel. Gaines v. Canada*. (S. W. Canada was the registrar at the University of Missouri.) Houston appealed the case, however, until it landed on the docket of the United States Supreme Court. Houston put a great amount of hope in the Gaines case, believing that, if successful, the Missouri case could become a "key to the NAACP effort to desegregate schools nationwide."[23] His intent and purpose was to establish a framework in support of the "argument that if no separate but equal schools existed for black students, there is no option but integration."[24] The Supreme Court made its decision in December 1938. It came as something of a surprise that the Supreme Court ruled that the University of Missouri was required to enroll Gaines into its law school. Houston was ecstatic. For the court, the laws of Missouri had denied Gaines his guarantee of equal rights under the Fourteenth Amendment. In the words of Chief Justice Charles Evans Hughes, the Missouri laws were unconstitutional because only black residents of the state were required to "go outside the state to obtain" a degree in law.[25] The *Murray* decision had impacted the state of Maryland, but the *Gaines* case would have a national impact.

The following year, significant change came to the New York headquarters of the NAACP. Houston had decided that it was time for him to leave the organization and take up law practice as a partner with his father. With his departure in the spring of

With the help of attorney Charles Houston, Lloyd Gaines was eventually granted admission to the University of Missouri's law school by the U.S. Supreme Court. Mysteriously, not long after the decision, Gaines vanished while running an errand and never attended the school.

MARSHALL, A MISSISSIPPI YOUTH, AND AN ORANGE

Few black lawyers carried a higher sense of cause and purpose toward the struggle for civil rights during the twentieth century than Thurgood Marshall. For decade after decade, Marshall, together with other lawyers working for the NAACP, led the crusade to right the wrongs of racism across America. He had not started out with such noble causes in mind, however. During his college years, before law school, Marshall was not known for taking his studies seriously, but he was known for playing pranks and practical jokes. Racial issues were unimportant to the young collegian. Even after he graduated from law school, he had not yet gained a sense of moral purpose regarding the struggle felt by so many blacks in America who were not afforded such opportunities. What, then, gave Thurgood Marshall his sense of injustice and the lifelong drive to fight against the long odds of racism that were often sanctioned by the law? It could be said that Marshall changed his attitude because of a piece of fruit—an orange.

After his graduation from the Howard Law School in May 1933, young Marshall emerged a serious student, although he had not yet decided on a direction for his legal career. During his years as a law student, however, he did gain tremendous respect for Charles Houston, the law school's dean. Houston was a man of principle and high expectations, and Marshall, who had buckled down in law school, had worked hard to please Houston. "I'd got the horsin' around out of my system and I heard law books were to dig in so I dug deep," Marshall noted years later.* His efforts had already paid off: By graduation, Houston had taken notice of Marshall, who had become the top student in his class. In fact, while Marshall was still a student, Houston invited him to work on some legal matters for the NAACP.

The summer after graduation, Houston took Marshall along with him on a fact-finding tour of the poor conditions of black schools across the South. At the time, the NAACP was considering challenging segregation in public schools by filing a legal suit. Through those hot, summer weeks, Houston and young Marshall, traveling in Houston's car, examined many southern schools, reaching destinations as far from Maryland as New Orleans. Finding themselves moving within the world of southern "Jim Crow" laws, Houston and Marshall faced constant prejudice, "staying in private homes and eating whatever greasy food they could get since they could not go into Jim Crow restaurants."** The two men often bought food, especially bags of fresh fruit, and kept it in the car to make certain they would have something to eat at all times.

The two lawyers found conditions in black schools appalling. During an inspection of a run-down rural school in Mississippi, Marshall had an epiphany—he experienced an event that would change his life. The school was abysmal. Intended for the children of poor black sharecroppers, the school was nothing more than a dilapidated shack, similar to the homes of blacks in that region of the Mississippi Delta. As Houston continued to examine the poor conditions of the school, young Marshall took some of the food out of the car and began to eat his lunch. One of the local black boys came by and watched Marshall as he ate an orange. At first, Marshall was put off, certain the boy was staring at him. Then, he realized that the boy was looking at his orange. He reached into the car and handed an orange to the young stranger, who promptly bit into it, rind and all. Then, Marshall had another realization: "He had never seen an orange before. He just bit right through it and enjoyed it."*** The scene would have a profound effect on the previously directionless young lawyer. "Marshall did not know exactly what a lawyer could do about racists and poor black kids living in such deprived conditions that an orange was an exotic fruit. But for the first time he wanted to do something, and do it soon."†

---

* Quoted in Juan Williams, *Thurgood Marshall: American Revolutionary*. New York: Three Rivers Press, 1998, p. 56.
** Quoted in Williams, *Thurgood Marshall*, p. 60.
*** Ibid.
† Ibid.

1939, Thurgood Marshall stepped into his shoes. Marshall soon set out to change the direction of the legal offices of the NAACP. He helped establish the Legal Defense and Educational Fund, Inc. (LDF), "to render free legal aid to Negroes who suffer legal injustice because of their race."[26] Marshall and other NAACP officials had been compelled to separate its legal activities from the main organization, because the IRS was threatening to deny the NAACP's tax-exempt status, since it was actively involved in political efforts to push antilynching legislation through Congress. As a separate organization, the LDF could avoid taking direct political stands, such as lobbying for specific laws, and thus remain a nonprofit organization. As the NAACP's Special Counsel, Marshall directed the work of the LDF.

Over the 10 ten years, Marshall led the efforts of the LDF (under the direction of the NAACP) in its fight against the discrepancies of "separate but equal." In 1939, he took on a Maryland county school board for its practice of paying black teachers less than white teachers. When he won his case, black teachers received significant raises across the state. He managed the same success in Virginia in 1940. Through these successes, the cause of civil rights advanced even as Marshall's career was taking off:

> By this time, Marshall was gaining a national reputation. He became known as "Mr. Civil Rights," a brilliant and tireless lawyer who roamed the nation fighting key civil rights battles in court. He defended blacks accused of crimes. He argued highly technical cases involving subtle aspects of constitutional law. Often he conducted his business in the courtrooms of small Southern towns, where the local citizens did not take a liking to brilliant black men who fought for the legal and civil rights of beaten-down black citizens. Marshall was fearless, though, shaking off threats on his life with a joke or an amusing anecdote.[27]

Although Houston had laid the groundwork for such efforts in the name of the NAACP and black rights, Marshall was taking the work of civil rights to new levels.

4

Marshall Takes the Reins

Perhaps because of the groundbreaking civil rights work that Houston had done and that Marshall continued on behalf of the NAACP, change appeared to be taking place even beyond the scope of their particular cases. In 1939, a black professor from Howard University's law school, James Nabrit, won a case involving an Oklahoma law designed to keep blacks from voting. The case, *Lane v. Wilson*, was won by a 6 to 2 decision of the U.S. Supreme Court. The court accepted Nabrit's argument that the Oklahoma statute was a violation of the Fifteenth Amendment, which guaranteed the vote to American citizens. Two years later, the Supreme Court decided *Mitchell v. United*

States, citing against an Arkansas statute that required blacks to ride in railroad passenger cars without running water or toilet facilities. In 1944, Thurgood Marshall himself argued the case *Smith v. Allwright* before the Supreme Court and successfully brought about the end of a Texas law that also denied blacks the right to vote in primary elections. Two years later, Marshall was again tearing down legal barricades, winning the case of

A student of Charles Houston, Thurgood Marshall (1908–1993) continued his work for the NAACP. Marshall fought and won many groundbreaking cases and later became the first African American to serve on the U.S. Supreme Court.

Morgan v. Virginia. The Supreme Court accepted his arguments on behalf of Irene Morgan, a black woman from Virginia who refused to sit on the back seat of a bus to Baltimore and was subsequently arrested and fined. The court agreed that Virginia law did not apply to interstate transportation.

These general cases helped the cause in opposition to Jim Crow laws, and Thurgood Marshall remained in the thick of the fight. Although he was working on cases involving interstate transportation and black voting rights, he did not abandon the struggle to eliminate segregation from higher education. During the late 1940s, Marshall became actively involved in a pair of cases involving two black men wanting to attend graduate schools in states where such programs were segregated: Herman Marion Sweatt, a mail carrier from Texas, and George W. McLaurin, a 68-year-old teacher.

Marshall became involved first in the Sweatt case. His client had applied for acceptance into the University of Texas School of Law and was rejected because he was black. Marshall and Sweatt sued the Texas school, and a local court ordered the university to either admit Sweatt or open a separate school of law equal to its existing school for black students. When the University of Texas made a half-hearted effort (the black law school had no library, and consisted of a few rented rooms in a small town outside Houston, and two professors), the county court was pleased, but Marshall and Sweatt were not. Marshall appealed the case to a higher court, intending to bring about "a real showdown fight against Jim Crow education."[28] It would not be an easy case to win. The president of the University of Texas, Theophilus Shickel Painter, was determined he would not allow blacks to enter his university. The case would bear his name: *Sweatt v. Painter.*

Painter intended to cut off Sweatt's case by creating a "separate but equal" law school for black students. Even before the appeals court sat to hear the case, Painter made public his plans to build the new black law school. It would be much larger and better staffed and equipped than the slap-dab school that had been thrown together outside Houston at Prairie View. Once the case was presented, the university's lawyers argued that a "separate but equal" school would soon be available, and they criticized Marshall for pursuing the case, claiming it "was merely being fought for the benefit of the NAACP, not because the plaintiff really desired a legal education."[29] Marshall was prepared to play the high-stakes game the university wanted to play. During testimony, he presented an expert witness, Professor Robert Redfield, from the University of Chicago's anthropology department. Redfield testified that black students were just as intelligent as white students and that, if given the same educational opportunities and advantages, would match white students academically. The Texas Court of Appeals did not accept Marshall's arguments and sided with the university, stating that the new black law school satisfied the tenets of "separate but equal." Marshall, of course, did not give up the case. Over the next three years, he managed to get the case heard before the U.S. Supreme Court.

In the meantime, Marshall took on another higher education case, this time involving an elderly teacher, George McLaurin, who had been turned down by the University of Oklahoma strictly because of his race. (McLaurin was trying to enter the doctoral program in education.) Marshall filed the suit in a U.S. district court, which decided in McLaurin's favor. It ordered the university to admit the black teacher. All was still not well yet, though, even after that. McLaurin, while attending classes, was required to sit separately from the white students in a row marked "Reserved for Colored." He was only allowed to sit at one specific table in the law library and ate at his own designated table in the university cafeteria. Marshall stepped in again, informing the Oklahoma district court of McLaurin's treatment. The court did nothing on McLaurin's behalf. Marshall took the case to the U.S. Supreme Court. The high court was scheduled to hear the case in April 1950, the same day it would hear the details of the Sweatt case.

When George McLaurin was finally admitted to the University of Oklahoma thanks to the efforts of Thurgood Marshall, he was forced to sit separately from the other students in the class. Marshall was forced to take the case to the U.S. Supreme Court.

Many people knew it was an important case that Marshall was going to present to the Supreme Court that spring day in 1950. In his brief to the court, Marshall had argued that laws that required segregation in schools in a given state did harm to blacks. He requested that the concept of "separate but equal" be struck down as an equalizer before the law.

With the future of the *Plessy v. Ferguson* precedent possibly on the line, the courtroom was packed that day:

Hundreds of people stood in line for hours outside the Supreme Court hoping to get a seat to hear the case argued in April 1950. Those who were lucky enough to get in saw Marshall make an emotional argument, asserting that Sweatt had a right to attend the state law school without regard to how white segregationists might feel or objections from blacks. "The rights of Sweatt to attend the University of Texas cannot be conditioned upon the wishes of any group of citizens," Marshall told the justices. "It matters not to me whether every single Negro in this country wants segregated schools. It makes no difference whether every white person wants segregated schools. If Sweatt wants to assert his individual, constitutional right, it cannot be conditioned upon the wishes of every other citizen."[30]

In response, Marshall's opposition, Texas Attorney General Price Daniel argued that "if Sweatt were admitted to the law school, then blacks would have to be admitted to swimming pools, grammar schools, and hospitals."[31]

Marshall and the NAACP waited nearly two months for the Supreme Court's justices to render their decision. In the interval, Marshall was handed some devastating news. His old mentor, Charles Houston, had died of heart failure in Washington, D.C. While Marshall and Houston had not maintained constant contact with one another as they had in early days, the blow to Marshall was significant. Houston had served an invaluable role in the early career of the young lawyer from Maryland, and their relationship, both personal and public, "had evolved from that of mentor and student to professional confidants."[32] Houston had been instrumental in Marshall's presentation of the Sweatt case to the court, having told Marshall to take the "direct attack approach."[33] When Houston's funeral was held, Marshall and other NAACP leaders, including Walter White and Roy Wilkins, together with a pair of Supreme Court justices, Hugo Black and Tom Clark, shared pews in Howard University's Rankin Chapel. During the service, Houston's leadership for the cause of black civil rights in America was likened to that of Moses.

Five weeks later, on June 5, 1950, the Supreme Court handed down its decision in the case of *Sweatt v. Painter*. The decision had been unanimous and much to Marshall's liking. The court sided with Sweatt. The justices felt that the new law school for blacks did not present a "legal education equivalent to that offered by the state to students of other races."[34] In every key way that a law school might distinguish itself, the justices stated—by its faculty, administration, alumni status, history, community standing, prestige—the black law school was lacking. By including these

THE DISAPPEARANCE OF LLOYD GAINES

In 1938, the Supreme Court's decision in favor of Lloyd Gaines was considered a major victory on the part of Houston and his NAACP legal team. The long-range impact did not materialize as Houston had hoped, however. One of the major impediments to that ultimate effect proved to be Lloyd Gaines himself.

The 28-year-old Gaines prepared to enroll in the law school at the Missouri University in the spring of 1939, just as the 1938 Supreme Court decision had authorized him to do. The state of Missouri still attempted to thwart the decision and Gaines's intentions. Hurriedly, state officials authorized the construction of a law school at Lincoln University in the state capital, Jefferson City. This would have provided a Jim Crow alternative at best. State legislators argued that "with separate and equal facilities available to Gaines, there was no need to admit him to the University of Missouri."* Houston and the NAACP legal team leapt back into action and returned to a Missouri court to once again argue on behalf of Gaines. The new law school at Lincoln was not yet open, Houston argued, and Gaines was ready to enroll in law school. A lower Missouri court decided against Gaines, and the Missouri State Supreme Court agreed. The NAACP would need to continue fighting Gaines's fight.

Gaines, however, had had enough of the legal proceedings that ultimately only managed to delay his plans to attend law school. In addition, he began to act poorly. Gaines "wanted the NAACP to treat him criteria in making its decision, the Supreme Court managed to redefine the standard for "separate but equal," which created a rippling effect. Using additional benchmarks of the quality of a school, such as its alumni and the school's prestige and influence, as well as its long-term historical impact, the court was

like a star."** He began throwing tantrums. He knew the NAACP needed him to continue its crusade against "separate but equal." He asked for money from the civil rights organization so he could begin attending school while the courts considered whether the new law school under construction at Lincoln University was adequate or not. Frustrated NAACP officials paid for Gaines to attend the University of Michigan, where he began pursuing a master's degree in economics. Then, sometime during the spring of 1939, Lloyd Gaines simply disappeared. What exactly happened to Gaines still remains a mystery. Some said he was killed, but there did not appear to be any evidence of it. Others claimed that he had been bribed to drop out of the NAACP's case. According to one black newspaper columnist, "Gaines had sent a postcard from Mexico to a friend and was having 'a jolly time on the $2,000 he had been given to leave the country.'"***

Whatever the situation concerning Gaines' disappearance, it caused the NAACP's efforts on his behalf to grind to a halt. With this setback, after having spent years in support of Gaines, Charles Hamilton Houston made a decision in April 1939 to leave the NAACP's legal offices. He was gone by July and replaced by Thurgood Marshall.

* Quoted in Juan Williams, *Thurgood Marshall: American Revolutionary*. New York: Three Rivers Press, 1998, p. 97.
** Ibid.
*** Ibid., p. 98.

Herman Marion Sweatt is pictured walking on the campus of the University of Texas School of Law, in Austin, Texas, after the U.S. Supreme Court granted him permission to attend the formerly segregated school.

setting a new standard. With these criteria, "no makeshift Jim Crow school could ever be presented as a facility 'equal' to a long-standing state school."[35]

The majority decision read much as the LDF lawyer had hoped:

> We cannot find substantial equality in the educational opportunities offered white and Negro law students by the state. . . . The University of Texas Law School is far superior. . . . A law school, the proving ground for legal learning and practice, cannot be effective in isolation. . . . Anyone who has practiced law, would not choose to study in an academic

vacuum, removed from the play of ideas and the exchange of views with which the law is concerned.[36]

The decision was singularly important. With Marshall's previous wins with the *Murray v. Maryland* and *Gaines v. Canada* cases, his clients had gained admittance to white law schools where no black alternative was available. With this new decision, Marshall had managed to convince the Supreme Court to admit a black student to an all-white school even though a law school for blacks, albeit an inferior one, was available.

Marshall would experience a dual victory that summer day in 1950. The court also handed down their decision in Marshall's other case, *McLaurin v. Oklahoma State Regents for Higher Education*. In this decision, the court ruled that the restrictions put on McLaurin by the Oklahoma university had managed to "impair and inhibit his ability to study, to engage in discussion and exchange views with other students, and in general, to learn his profession."[37] The court's ruling also recognized that, should McLaurin be kept in his previous state of learning, the result would be a cycle of impairment, since any students he might one day teach "will necessarily suffer to the extent that his training is unequal to that of his classmates."[38] The Supreme Court having spoken, McLaurin had received the green light to enroll in the University of Oklahoma with no more restrictions placed on him than were applied to white students.

Marshall had no choice but to savor this pair of satisfactory Supreme Court decisions. There would be great celebrating in the offices of the NAACP, and Marshall could be found in the middle of the hoopla. As one of the organization's members noted: "Thurgood, he's a party man. You would not have to have much of an excuse for him to throw a party."[39] Marshall also understood that the twin victories on behalf of Sweatt and McLaurin were not ends in themselves, though; rather, they were the next link in a chain of events that would one day bring extraordinary change to the world of America's blacks. The Supreme Court had opened the doors of whites-only universities and allowed blacks to matriculate. The issue in both cases had centered on the concept of "separate but equal." Marshall's next goal would be to make the case that the system of segregated schools in America was designed to provide an inadequate education for blacks. By 1950, the legacy of "separate but equal," and its continuing impact—more than a half century's worth—of *Plessy v. Ferguson* seemed closer to an end.

EQUAL·JUSTICE·UNDER·LAW·

5

A Pair of Important Cases

By 1950, Thurgood Marshall was a legend among black civil rights leaders in America. With the Sweatt and McLaurin victories, the 42-year-old Marshall had successfully argued 10 race-related cases before the U.S. Supreme Court. Following those decisions, Marshall believed he could see light at the end of a very dark and long tunnel: "The complete destruction of all enforced segregation is now in sight. . . . Segregation no longer has the stamp of legality in any public education."[40] In black publications and newspapers, Marshall "was trumpeted as the one man able to defend black Americans against the Klan, racist judges, and bigoted small-town cops."[41] Blacks across the South began to understand that, if Marshall became involved in one of their cases, it had a good chance of being successful. Among southern blacks a phrase was created, one that signaled "the day when the sword of justice would strike out against white oppressors: 'Thurgood's coming.'"[42]

With each legal decision, Marshall and his colleagues succeeded in removing a single brick in the wall of government-sanctioned segregation, and the legacy of *Plessy v. Ferguson* was beginning to crumble. Marshall was not content with the progress, though. He did not want to spend his entire legal career chipping away at "separate but equal." He wanted it destroyed; he wanted it gone.

Although the work of Marshall and the NAACP was proving crucial, it appeared that change relative to segregation was taking place on other fronts, as well. President Truman had officially ordered the desegregation of the armed forces by the late 1940s. In the social arena of professional sports, the Brooklyn Dodgers had hired a World War II veteran, a black infielder named Jackie Robinson, to its minor league team in Montreal. Two years later, in 1947, Robinson was playing for the Dodgers in New York. Soon other baseball teams were signing on black athletes. For an increasing number of Americans, the color barrier and segregation was out-of-date and out-of-step for a nation that had just recently gone to war to defeat Hitler and National Socialism, a rabid political philosophy that had led to the extermination of millions of innocent people simply because of their race.

As for Marshall, he did not bask for long in the warm sunshine of his back-to-back Supreme Court victories. There were other cases to try, and by the early 1950s, the NAACP was actively involved in four additional lawsuits, each of which focused on school segregation. (Several of these cases dated back to the 1940s, when Marshall first took an interest in them.) Two of them stemmed from circumstances at schools in the South, including South Carolina and Virginia. The third was a Delaware case, and the fourth was centered in Topeka, Kansas. Together, they would ultimately lead to one of the most monumental race cases of the twentieth century.

THE *BRIGGS V. ELLIOTT* CASE

The *Briggs v. Elliott* case opened in 1947, in the school system of Clarendon County, South Carolina. The structure of the county school system was typical of those found across the South. Black students attended classes in little more than wooden shacks covered over with tar paper. Some of these schools had actually been built by local churches. There was almost no money available for educating the county's black children. Many did not attend school because the distance from their homes to a

Due to a lack of state funds, many African American schools fell far short of the equality mandated by *Plessy v. Ferguson*. This South Carolina schoolhouse, photographed in 1938, is an example of the type of facility that brought about the *Briggs v. Elliott* case.

school was too great. Some students had to walk as far as eight miles to their classes, because there was no school bus available. When a legal suit was eventually filed, the issue was the school's busing policy.

The school board had authorized the use of 34 school buses to deliver white students to school but none for black students. Black parents, led by a black minister, Joseph Albert DeLaine (who was also the principal for the St. Paul Rural Primary School, attended by black students), requested the school board to provide buses for their children. The school board said no. School officials told DeLaine that black students were not provided a bus because their parents did not pay enough taxes to pay for one. DeLaine and his supporters then appealed to state officials; again, they were denied. For a time, black parents across the county relied on an old bus they had purchased themselves, but when it broke down, there was no money to fix it. It was then that DeLaine and others decided to take their case to court. When the case went to court, however, it was thrown out because of a simple technicality: The court determined that the case's plaintiff lived on the line between the school district of Clarendon County and a neighboring county.

The situation in Clarendon County in time came into the view of the NAACP and Thurgood Marshall. By March, 1949, he made a trip to Clarendon County where he met with local black leaders and parents. Marshall discovered the lopsided condition of schools for blacks compared to whites. The county school board spent nearly $180 annually on each white student (about $1,480 today), while only spending about $40 per black student (about $330 today). Teachers in the white schools taught an average of 28 students. Teachers in the county's black schools were responsible for nearly 50. The schools Marshall toured were vastly inferior, and they had no indoor plumbing. Black students were even charged a fee for coal used to heat their schools, whereas white students were not asked to make similar payments. Marshall encouraged the group to allow the NAACP to file a lawsuit on their behalf in response to "the grossly unequal educational facilities provided for Clarendon County's black students."[43] The case would bear the names of one of the county's black parents, Harry Briggs, who was a navy veteran and father of five school-age children, and the school board chairman, R. W. Elliott. Eighteen other blacks joined the suit along with Briggs. The case would be presented before a three-judge panel.

On May 28, 1951, Marshall brought the case *Briggs v. Elliott* before the U.S. district court in Charleston, the state capital. Hundreds of black families were present in the courtroom that day, ready to hear Thurgood Marshall speak on their behalf. Many had never been inside a courtroom before, but they wanted to see the NAACP attorney they had heard so much about. At the heart of Marshall's presentation to the court was his insistence that the school officials of Clarendon County had not created an educational system that was equal between the races. The facts on that point were so clear and obvious that the school board's attorney, Robert Figg, agreed in court. Figg, "a tall studious man in a white suit,"[44] stated that the governor of South Carolina was aware of the problem and that he was "proposing sweeping legislation and significant expenditures that would remedy the situation."[45] Figg contended that the case should be halted until the state of South Carolina had had time to repair its educational system. Marshall, however, who had seen this type of tactic before, would not accept the "intentions" and "plans" of the state of South Carolina. Besides, argued Marshall, it would take at least $40 million to make the black schools in South Carolina equal to those of white students. The case should be looked at according to the facts at hand. Marshall would not give in to promises of better schools for blacks that did not include ending the segregationist policies found in South Carolina. He intended to strike a blow against "separate but equal," not be a part of patching up a bad system. Marshall's intention to make the *Briggs v. Elliott* case a struggle over the future of segregation in public schools remained a hard fight. Figg argued that *Plessy v. Ferguson* and its concept of "separate but equal" was still law, and he even hinted that his state might decide not to collect taxes earmarked for schools if South Carolina was ordered to desegregate its school system.

Presenting the facts of the *Briggs v. Elliott* case took a day and a half. The three-judge panel deliberated for three weeks before rendering a decision. In fact, the court made two decisions. The

DOLLS IN THE COURTROOM

One of Marshall's goals in presenting his case for *Briggs v. Elliott* was to argue that segregation gave black students a poor psychological view of themselves; that the entire policy of "separate but equal" left them damaged—not just in having received an inferior education, but that it skewed their view of what it meant to be black in America. To that end, he called an expert witness to the stand. Kenneth Clark was a black psychologist from City College of New York who, along with his wife, Mamie, had carried out a unique study of the damage caused by segregation. Clark's study had incorporated the use of black and white dolls:

> He would show a child a black doll and a white doll and ask the child which he or she liked best, which doll was nicer, which doll was more fun to play with. . . . More often than not, black children identified the white doll as being nicer and more fun to play with. . . . Clark concluded, therefore, that black children, even youngsters three or four years old, had already developed a negative self-image. He reasoned that their disliking of the black dolls indicated their dissatisfaction with their own racial background, a dissatisfaction resulting from living in a segregated society that judged black people as inferiors.*

Before the case went to court, Dr. Clark carried out a local version of his study, asking 16 black children from Clarendon County their presiding judge, John J. Parker, issued the court's decision and announced that South Carolina would be required to provide equal schools to black students. The court gave the state six months to make adjustments, then report back to the court. The court, however, by a vote of 2 to 1, did not agree to Marshall's call for an end to segregation. The court's majority cited that segregated schools had existed for 75 years and that "it is a late day to say that such segregation is violative of fundamental

opinions about the black and white dolls. Of the 16 children, 11 said they thought the black doll was bad and 10 considered the white doll as "nicer." As a witness, he testified that, in his professional opinion, he believed the "children, in Clarendon County, like other human beings who are subjected to an obviously inferior status in which they live, have been definitely harmed in the development of their personalities."**
Marshall himself drew his own conclusions during his summation to the court, stating: "The Negro child is made to go to an inferior school; he is branded in his own mind as inferior. This sets up a roadblock in his mind which prevents his ever feeling he is equal. You can teach such a child a Constitution, anthropology, and citizenship, but he knows it isn't true."***

Marshall spoke out against continuing the segregationist policy of "separate but equal." It was a practice he considered unlawful and the only answer was to abolish *Plessy v. Ferguson*: "There is no relief for the Negro children of Clarendon County except to be permitted to attend existing and superior white schools."†

* Quoted in James Tackach, *Brown v. Board of Education*. San Diego: Lucent Books, 1998, p. 47.
** Ibid.
*** Ibid., p. 48.
† Ibid.

Harry Briggs, Jr. (second row, at right) is photographed with his schoolmates in South Carolina in 1953.

constitutional rights."[46] The dissenting voice on the court, Judge Julius Waties Waring, wrote otherwise, citing his belief that "segregation in education can never produce equality."[47] Marshall considered the court's decision as a loss. Segregation was still intact in the schools of South Carolina.

The case played itself out in various other ways in Clarendon County. In response to the lawsuit, local whites began persecuting anyone they knew had been involved in the case. DeLaine was fired from his job as school principal. His house and church were both burned by arsonists, and the local fire department did nothing to put out the blazes. Eventually, DeLaine was hounded from the county. Others involved in the lawsuit suffered similar intimidations. Even Judge Waring, who had spoken against segregation, was treated with contempt. The South Carolina House of Representatives criticized Waring, and he eventually left the state after receiving death threats. As for Briggs, he, too, had to leave South Carolina and take a job in Florida, for years living separate from his family, sending them money. In an interview, Briggs's wife, Eliza, explained what her husband's involvement in the court case meant to her family: "It was really sad for my family. My children didn't have their daddy around. He said if it didn't help our children, it would help the rest of the children coming along."[48]

The decision by the South Carolina court would not be the last word for *Briggs v. Elliott*, though. Marshall and his colleagues appealed the case in the summer of 1951. They intended to use it to their advantage in connection with other similar cases before the U.S. Supreme Court.

A LITTLE GIRL IN TOPEKA

The same week the South Carolina court rendered its decision in the *Briggs v. Elliott* case, another school segregation case was beginning to take shape hundreds of miles away, in the state of Kansas. A federal district court judge began hearing arguments in a case that had been filed on behalf of a seven-year-old black girl named Linda Brown. During the fall of the previous year,

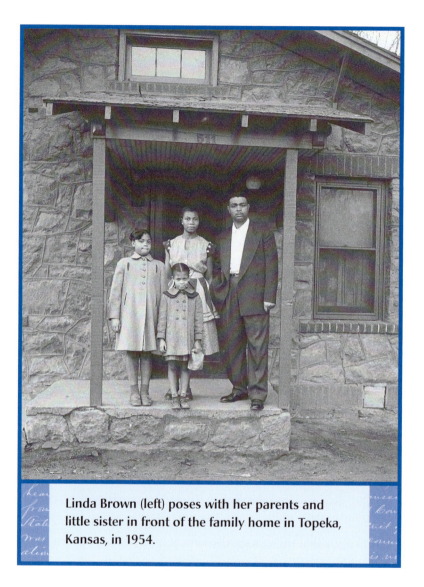

Linda Brown (left) poses with her parents and little sister in front of the family home in Topeka, Kansas, in 1954.

young Linda had entered the first grade. She lived in a poor neighborhood of Topeka, where the children she played with were of various races: black, Latino, white. Every morning, the first-grader had to walk two miles to the place where a school bus picked her up to take her another five miles to the Monroe Elementary School. The Monroe school was not even close to Linda Brown's neighborhood. The white children in her neighborhood, however, attended a school much closer to where Linda lived, Sumner School, just seven blocks away.

Linda's father, Reverend Oliver Brown, weary of the difficulties and challenges his daughter faced every weekday to get to a school that was so far away and inferior, finally had enough. He joined a group of other dissatisfied blacks in the Topeka NAACP who had been working since 1948 to convince the city's school board to, if not abandon its policy of segregation, at least improve the existing black schools. When the group made no progress, its members decided to pursue a lawsuit. The New York headquarters office was contacted, requesting a suit be filed. Reverend Brown agreed to have his name placed on the suit at the top of the list of plaintiffs. (His name came first alphabetically.) In joining the suit, Brown was not intent on pursuing the larger goals of the NAACP regarding segregation in public schools. The local minister "was an ordinary citizen who was angered that his daughter had to travel each day past a modern, fully equipped white school to a black school housed in a deteriorated building."[49]

When Marshall was contacted about the case, he was already at work on the Clarendon County case. A pair of LDF lawyers, Robert Carter and Jack Greenberg, were dispatched to Topeka to take on the case. Late in June 1951, the case appeared before a three-judge panel of the U.S. District Court for the state of Kansas. Reverend Brown and other black parents from Topeka were in the courtroom. Unlike so many other school cases, the focus of the *Brown* case was not about the poor conditions of the school or a lack of equipment, buses, or facilities. In many ways, the black schools in Topeka were not dramatically different from the white schools. For this case, Carter and Greenberg, along with local lawyers John and Charles Scott and Charles Bledsoe, took the position that the problem was that the city of Topeka had segregated schools at all—that segregation put an unfair and undue burden on black students and that the entire system was unfairly tipped against them.

When the *Brown* case received its hearing in the summer of 1951, it came at a time when "Topeka and the state of Kansas had a schizophrenic attitude about its Negro population."[50] There was legal and practiced segregation in Kansas, to be sure. It was not to be found in every school district in the state, however. Unlike the southern states, Kansas's black population was relatively small, less than 8 percent of the state's total population. Although many of the state's blacks were poor, they were not universally discriminated against. Blacks in Topeka were sometimes able to join and become members of the same public organizations and civic clubs that whites joined. As for hotels and public eating establishments in the city, they were typically segregated, but this was not the case for Topeka's bus and train stations. If a black family wanted to go out and see a motion picture, they might find it difficult. Five of the city's seven movie houses were segregated, while one was a black theater and the seventh was integrated. Under Kansas state law, there was no mandate for segregation in public schools. Institutions of higher learning, such as Washburn and the University of Kansas were already integrated and had been for many years. As for elementary and secondary schools, the state left the decision of segregation up to the cities themselves.

BROWN RECEIVES A HEARING

The timing of the *Brown* case in district court proved a little awkward. The *Briggs* case had not yet been decided, and the LDF was uncertain how important and effective expert witnesses would prove to be. (The *Briggs* case ended just a month before the *Brown* case was scheduled to open.) Also, with a summer date for the case's hearing, it proved difficult to find experts such as professors available. Carter and Greenberg were able to collar several, however, including Dr. Hugh Speer, the chair of the Education Department at the University of Kansas City. Speer had done a study of the schools, both black and white, in Topeka, and his study had found "in each case that the white schools were newer or otherwise physically superior to the black schools."[51] In his testimony, Speer addressed the impact of segregation on black students:

> If the colored children are denied the experience of associating with white children, who represent 90 percent of our national society in which these colored children must live, then the colored child's curriculum is being greatly curtailed. The Topeka curriculum or any school curriculum cannot be equal under segregation.[52]

Additional expert testimony was provided by a psychology professor from Ohio State University, Horace B. English, who stated that the learning ability of blacks was no different than that of whites, but that the expectations of society had a strong influence on black learning. Segregation, said English, was a clear sign to black students that they did not count as much as white students and were not expected to succeed academically, and that such obvious differences between black and white schools led black children to think of themselves as inferior. Another professor of psychology, Louisa Holt, who taught at Kansas University, provided parallel testimony to English's, but she went on to make an additional and extremely crucial point about the impact segregated schools had on black students:

> The fact that it is enforced, that it is legal, I think, has more importance than the mere fact of segregation by itself does because this gives legal and official sanction to a policy which is inevitably interpreted both by white people and by Negroes as denoting the inferiority of the Negro group.[53]

Professor Holt's point was clear: Laws allowing segregated schools to exist were as bad as the schools themselves. The existence of such laws confirmed what many whites believed: that blacks were inferior.

Despite having presented a solid case on behalf of their clients, Carter and Greenberg failed to win over the three-judge panel. By early August, the judges announced their decision. In taking on a case in Topeka, the NAACP had taken a long shot at destroying segregation. The court stated that "Topeka's segregated schools were, for the most part, of comparable quality."[54] Therefore, the school system was in general agreement with *Plessy v. Ferguson's* mandate calling for "separate but equal." It was the court's opinion that "the physical facilities, the curricula, courses of study, qualifications of and quality of teachers, as well as other educational facilities in the two sets of schools are comparable."[55] As such, the court continued, the civil and constitutional rights of the black students in the Topeka system had not been denied.

This issue of equality of facilities had not been the primary point made by the NAACP legal team, but it was a ruling that the NAACP would be able to use to its advantage in appealing the judges' decision. In previous public school cases filed by the NAACP's LDF, there had been important differences between the white schools and black schools in a given county or city. This was not true in Topeka. When the case was sent to the Supreme Court for appeal, it would allow the high court to rule "in the NAACP's favor on the equality issue without a resolution of whether segregation itself violated the Constitution."[56] The Supreme Court would have to deal with the important question of whether segregation could be allowed, given the equal protection clause of the Fourteenth Amendment.

The LDF's loss that day was no real surprise to its legal team. Carter and Greenberg had placed much of their emphasis on things that could not easily be proven, such as the claim that segregationist policies and law placed a strain on black students, resulting in their developing strong feelings of inferiority, which segregation policies were designed to create. The court had not sided with the NAACP lawyers' arguments—at least, not in their decision. It was not that the judges did not agree with the logic and its conclusion. In the court's written opinion, they stated: "Segregation of white and colored children in public schools has a detrimental [harmful] effect upon the colored children. The impact is greater when it has the sanction of the law; for the policy of separating the races is usually interpreted as denoting the inferiority of the Negro group."[57] They knew that *Plessy v. Ferguson* was the law of the land; that it would have to be the Supreme Court that struck down its own precedent.

In effect, the judges were handing the NAACP an opinion that would be useful in an appeal of their own decision. Speaking years later, one of the judges, Walter August Huxman, who was a judge for the Tenth Circuit Court of Appeals and a former Kansas governor, explained: "We weren't in sympathy with the decision we rendered [made]. If it weren't for *Plessy v. Ferguson*, we surely would have found the law unconstitutional. But there was no way around it—the Supreme Court had to overrule itself."[58] Robert Carter wasted almost no time filing the appeal he knew would constitute the next step in the NAACP's campaign to bring down "separate but equal." He filed on September 28, 1951.

6

The Battle Continues

The NAACP's legal strategy of jeopardizing *Plessy v. Ferguson's* legacy by filing multiple and overlapping cases marched forward, despite the initial loss of the *Brown* case. Next on their plate were a pair of cases emerging from the same state—Delaware. Both were filed with the Supreme Court in 1952: *Gebhart et al. v. Belton et al.* and *Gebhart v. Bulah.* In time, the two cases would be melded into one because their circumstances were so similar. The *Belton* case originated out of Wilmington, where two high schools, Claymont, the white school, and Howard High, the black school, served as clear contrasts in the educational opportunities represented.

Claymont was situated in a Wilmington suburb and was an affluent system where 400 students attended classes. Its lawns were finely manicured and its classrooms well equipped, and the school's program included special, advanced classes, as well as extracurricular activities. Across town stood Howard, the only black high school in the state, a school situated in an industrial part of Wilmington, dominated by the smokestacks of local factories and a warehouse district. Students from across town were delivered to Howard each day by bus. There were three times as many students per teacher at Howard than at Claymont. The inequality of the two systems was easy to see even at a casual glance.

The second Delaware case was the result of a white woman's protest against segregation. Sarah Bulah, who was white, lived in Hockessin, Delaware. She had adopted a young black girl years earlier. When that child came of age to go to school, she was required to attend a school for blacks. This required Bulah to drive her daughter across town to the black school, which was housed in a dilapidated old building, even as she passed a quality white school along the way. Both the *Bulah* and *Belton* cases were first taken on by the only black lawyer in the state of Delaware—Louis Redding. He worked out of the NAACP's Wilmington chapter. Redding had practiced law in Delaware since 1929 and was a graduate of Rice University and Harvard Law School. He was aided in presenting the joint cases by Jack Greenberg.

Redding and Greenberg filed their case in a Delaware state court. Originally, they had filed in a federal court, but the state's attorney general informed them that the laws in question were state laws and the case should be filed in a state court. This change was perfectly agreeable to the NAACP lawyers. They knew they would appear before Judge Collins Seitz who "had ruled in Louis Redding's favor in an earlier desegregation case involving the University of Delaware."[59] When both lawsuits

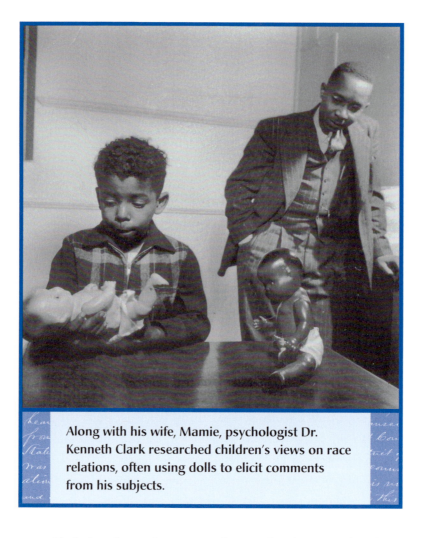

Along with his wife, Mamie, psychologist Dr. Kenneth Clark researched children's views on race relations, often using dolls to elicit comments from his subjects.

were filed, they bore the name of one of Wilmington's school board members—Francis Gebhart.

In presenting their case to Judge Seitz, Redding and Greenberg ushered a host of expert witnesses into the court room, 14 in all. They included Professor Otto Klineberg of Columbia University, who confirmed that the learning abilities of black and white students was equal. A psychologist testified concerning the ill-effects on black students of having to engage in lengthy bus rides every day to and from school. Educator and psychologist Dr. Kenneth Clark was called to the stand. He presented research he and his wife Mamie conducted with dolls that explored perception of race.

Although some of these witnesses appeared during previous school-related cases, this time was different. In this case, the experts testified about the effects of segregation policies and laws on white children. The study results presented in court argued that segregation bred prejudice: "In response to questions about how they felt about black children, some of the white students stated that they wanted to tie the hands of black students and force them to work. Others thought that black students should work when white students were allowed to play."[60] The state of Delaware offered no evidence or testimony to disprove the various claims made by these experts.

Such expert testimony before the court lasted for three days. Then, Judge Seitz paid a visit to both black and white schools to see for himself the general conditions of both. At one Wilmington black school, there was "no gymnasium, no nurse's office, and no water fountains. A single toilet accommodated the entire school—students and teachers alike."[61] Although much of the testimony and strategy employed in the two Delaware cases was similar to other NAACP cases, including the Clarendon County and Topeka cases, this time the court sided with the plaintiffs. In its April 1, 1952, decision, the court stated that "State-imposed segregation in education itself results in the Negro children, as a class, receiving educational opportunities which are substantially inferior to those available to white children similarly situated."[62] Judge Seitz's opinion was highly critical of Delaware law and its treatment of black students as second class. Seitz agreed with the experts who had testified, including Frederic Wertham, a well-known psychologist who had testified that "even if the black schools hired brilliant teachers like the great physicist Albert Einstein, those schools still would provide an inferior education."[63] Wertham had referred to segregation as "anti-educational."[64]

Seitz's decision went further than simply recognizing that segregation had resulted in creating a lopsided system

THURGOOD MARSHALL
TO THE FRONT

The U.S. Supreme Court handed Thurgood Marshall a pair of important legal victories—*Sweatt v. Painter* and *McLaurin v. Oklahoma State Regents for Higher Education*—on the same day: June 5, 1950. Although the decisions made headlines across America, they were swept off the front pages when war broke out in Korea. Within weeks, American forces, with the authorization of the United Nations, began arriving in South Korea to fight against communist forces.

These U.S. military units included both black and white troops. The U.S. military had maintained a segregationist policy in armed forces for many decades—through the Civil War, the Indian Wars, the Spanish-American War, and World Wars I and II. In 1948, just two years before the Korean War began, however, President and Commander-in-Chief Harry S. Truman ordered that all U.S. military troops be desegregated. All-black units still existed, however. One such unit (although it had white officers) was the U.S. 24th Infantry Regiment. The regiment won the first American victory in South Korea: Although the unit was grossly outnumbered, it retook the important city of Yechon during a battle that lasted for more than 16 hours.

Despite integration within the U.S. military, black troops were often treated poorly by white commanders, as well as by other enlisted men. During the early months of the Korean War, several black soldiers were tried for a variety of crimes, including rape, cowardice, general misbehavior, and failure to obey the orders of a superior officer. Although whites were accused of these crimes, too, the percentage of blacks accused was much higher than that of whites. Back in the states, the offices of the NAACP began to receive a barrage of complaints filed by black U.S. soldiers that they were being singled out and discriminated against. The complaints landed on Marshall's desk, and he soon noted that blacks were being court-martialed regularly, but white soldiers were not. Marshall made it clear that the NAACP was prepared to investigate the situation.

The NAACP sent Thurgood Marshall to Japan and Korea on a fact-finding mission. He interviewed court-martialed black soldiers and black soldiers in stockades awaiting military trial. He read the military records and legal transcripts of these soldiers, detecting a pattern of abuse. The trials of these black soldiers had been carried out by white officers and white military judges. Marshall found evidence of racism on the part of some of these military officials.

Through his investigation, Marshall discovered that, of the 82 cases that had resulted in general court-martial trials, the number of blacks accused was twice that of whites: 54 to 27. (One other case involved a soldier of Japanese descent.) He also discovered that 32 black soldiers had been convicted of "misbehavior in the face of the enemy,"* between August and October of 1950, while only two white soldiers had been similarly convicted. He also found that the blacks convicted had received harsher sentences, including one death sentence. Nearly half of the 32 were given a life sentence in prison. The two whites had received three- and five-year sentences, respectively.

When Marshall returned to the United States with his findings, he reported them to the press. Many Americans were immediately outraged. Congress soon called for an investigation. Soon, lawyers for the NAACP began representing blacks at the U.S. Army's Review Board. Through its efforts, the black civil rights group was able to get the sentences of 30 convicted black soldiers reduced and one sentence suspended completely.

* Quoted in D. J. Herda. *Thurgood Marshall: Civil Rights Champion*. Springfield, NJ: Enslow Publishers, 1995, p. 44.

of educating blacks and whites in Wilmington. He stated that the "separate but equal" concept should no longer be the norm between the races in public schools and that it would ultimately rest with the U.S. Supreme Court to reject the *Plessy v. Ferguson* maxim on a national scale. In the meantime, Seitz took a step in his decision that Thurgood Marshall would one day refer to as "the first real victory in our campaign to destroy segregation of American pupils in elementary and high schools."[65] He declared that the black students represented by the plaintiffs in both *Belton* and *Bulah* be admitted to the white schools closest to their local neighborhoods. It would no longer be the mandate in Wilmington to provide separate schools for its black students. Despite an appeal by the state, Judge Seitz's decision was upheld by the Delaware Supreme Court on August 28, 1952. The 1950s appeared to be shaping into the decade that would finally put *Plessy* and its racial legacy of the previous century out of business.

ONE MORE CASE

The early 1950s continued to bring additional cases for the NAACP to accept and take to court, all with the intention of striking down *Plessy v. Ferguson*. Another case arose in Virginia in 1951. That spring, the poor and inferior conditions at Moton High School, the black school in Prince Edward County, had become so unbearable that the entire student body of 450 decided to protest by going on strike and refusing to attend classes for two weeks. The students demanded that the local school board order the construction of a new school. When the board refused, some of the students wrote a letter to the NAACP's southeastern regional office in Richmond. The case fell into the hands of two LDF attorneys, Oliver Hill and Spottswood Robinson, both graduates of the Howard University School of Law. The two lawyers went to Prince Edward County to investigate conditions at the school. They met with the students and their parents at a local black church.

NAACP attorneys Spottswood Robinson (left) and Oliver Hill fought for desegregation of schools in Prince Edward County, Virginia, in the case *Davis v. County School Board of Prince Edward County*.

The small, rural community and its school "would not have been their choice for the location of a desegregation suit. . . . The lawyers preferred urban settings."[66] The students they met with, however, were determined. In response, the civil rights organization agreed to take on the Moton High students' cause. In the suit, which named all students at the high school, the new demand was not to build a new school, but to bring about the desegregation of the schools in Prince Edward County. The petition would bear the name of the first student on the lawyers' list of plaintiffs, a 14-year-old named Dorothy Davis. When the case reached the U.S. District Court in Richmond, it was titled *Davis v. County School Board of Prince Edward County.*

The five-day, three-judge case opened on May 23, 1951. Spottswood Robinson gave the opening oral arguments. He wanted the state of Virginia to alter its constitution by striking down its requirement for separate schools for blacks and whites. He and Hill presented a list of the poor conditions at Moton and insisted the court declare it inferior and unacceptable. As with other NAACP cases during these years, the lawyers brought in a group of expert witnesses who spoke about the psychological harm caused by segregation. A psychologist from Vassar College, M. Brewster Smith, testified on the harmful effects of segregated schools, arguing that such schools "make the Negro, on the average, more like the common, prejudiced conception of a Negro, as a stupid, illiterate, apathetic, but happy-go-lucky person."[67] Other expert witnesses testified, including Dr. Kenneth Clark, who again presented his famous doll study.

Despite the significant case made on behalf of their high school plaintiffs, the NAACP team was up against tough legal counsel. The Prince Edward County attorneys included Archibald Robertson, a partner in a prestigious Richmond law firm. Even the state's attorney general, James Almond, lent a hand to the defense. Almond, too, had visited the Moton High School facilities and found them sorely lacking. He knew it would be "impossible to defend the case on equivalency grounds."[68] The defense team would take another tack. Having studied the NAACP's approach to the recent case in Clarendon County, South Carolina, the defense decided to try and disprove the expert testimony presented by witnesses called by the LDF lawyers.

They pursued this strategy relentlessly. They cross-examined each professional witness intensely, attempting to discredit and even destroy his or her testimony. The defense lawyers also introduced experts of their own, some of whom challenged the expert testimony presented for the plaintiffs. One of those witnesses was Dr. Henry Garrett from Columbia University, who questioned the studies carried out by Dr. Clark. He stated that Clark's findings were questionable and that they were subject to other interpretations. He also testified that segregated schools did not harm black students. Local witnesses were presented as well. An additional strategy adopted by the defense was to argue that the citizens of Prince Edward, in segregating their schools, did so as a matter of social custom, not simply as a matter of law. This meant that, if the law was to change, bringing about desegregation, the people of the county and of Virginia in general would be unable to change. Defense attorneys even suggested, in the manner of a thinly veiled threat, that "Virginia would close its schools rather than comply with a desegregation order."[69] The Prince Edward County case proved to be one of the hardest fought by the NAACP during the late 1940s and early 50s.

The court handed down its decision on March 7, 1952. The school board had won its case. The court stated that the segregation practiced in Prince Edward County was "not arbitrary or capricious."[70] Instead, it was "one of the ways of life in Virginia. Separation of white and colored 'children' in the public schools of Virginia has for generations been a part of the mores of the people. To have separate schools has been their use and want."[71] As for the experts who testified concerning the impact and effect segregation had on black students, the court decided that it was not conclusive. That the Moton school was inadequate was never at issue on both sides, and the court ageed, ordering the county "to replace the Moton buildings and facilities with a new building and new equipment, or otherwise remove the inequality in them."[72] The court did not name a timetable for these mandated changes and improvements, only indicating that county officials were to remedy the problems "with diligence and dispatch."[73] Despite the disappointment of the NAACP and its lawyers, the *Davis v. County*

School Board of Prince Edward County would not wait long before being appealed.

HEADED FOR THE SUPREME COURT

The *Davis* decision had taken place in early March 1952. Over the next six months, a raft of NAACP-fought race and school cases were landing on the steps of the U.S. Supreme Court. By early May, LDF lawyers filed for a hearing of the *Briggs* case before the Supreme Court. A month later, the court responded, setting down both the *Briggs* case and the *Brown* case for possible argumentation during the court's fall term, which always opened in October. Then, by mid-July, the appeal for *Davis v. Prince Edward County* had been filed. The Delaware Supreme Court decided on the *Belton* and *Bulah* appeals and upheld the lower court's decision on August 28. Attorneys for the state filed an appeal of their own to the nation's high court. Throughout the summer of 1952, several legal roads were all converging on the same place.

Once the Supreme Court agreed to place *Briggs* and *Brown* on their fall docket, the lawyers at the NAACP began working around the clock to prepare their cases, many putting in 16-hour days, knowing the court represented their best and final hope. Through the second half of that summer, the New York office was a constant buzz of activity. Leading it all was Thurgood Marshall. No one knew better than Marshall the importance of these cases and their presentation to the Supreme Court. He had already spent years working on behalf of such cases, including the *Briggs* case directly, and, when he appeared before the court, it would constitute "the biggest case of his career."[74]

Marshall was intent on including all the best minds in the country that supported his and the NAACP's cause—dozens of lawyers and judges, law professors, sociologists, psychologists, even anthropologists. Disagreements over strategy developed. Some members of the NAACP legal team wanted to rely heavily on the sociology and psychology experts, whereas others wanted to present the case strictly from a legal standpoint. Marshall attempted the role of "peacemaker when the lawyers and the social scientists began sniping."[75] He wanted to rely on both. For him, despite his professionalism, the summer was a difficult, strenuous season of preparation. He was only 44 years old, but he was physically suffering. He lost sleep, making his heavy-lidded eyes appear puffy. He smoked too many Winston cigarettes. He gained weight. His marriage suffered as he spent long hours at the office, only coming home for any length of time on rare occasions.

The offices of the New York-based NAACP, however, were filled with a constant excitement that something good was going to happen:

> Conference rooms in the LDF's offices were crammed, often with sixty or more people standing and shouting. It was smoky, with Spott Robinson's pipe sending aromatic puffs into the air, followed by steady streams from Marshall's cigarettes and several cigars. Law books were strewn everywhere, and some people had to sit on the edges of tables because there weren't enough chairs. In the atmosphere tempers occasionally flared, and Marshall had to diffuse the tensions. Sometimes he would tell a joke. . .to get everyone laughing and back to work. . . . Despite the arguments and ego, Marshall, like the spirited conductor of a swing band, orchestrated lively meetings of legal talent. The meetings became renowned as great fun even though they involved hard work and little or no pay.[76]

Despite the ups and downs of so many professionals sharing crowded space, their ideas bouncing off the walls, it was a magical time within the New York offices of the NAACP. "It was an amazing feat to bring in black lawyers from the South and white lawyers and historians from the law schools," noted a law professor from Columbia University. "It almost became a national enterprise."[77]

IN THE UNITED STATES DISTRICT COURT FOR THE

EASTERN DISTRICT OF SOUTH CAROLINA

CHARLESTON DIVISION

FILED

MAY 9 1952

ERNEST L. ALLEN
C. B. C. U. S. E. B. S. C.

Civil Action No. 2657

HARRY BRIGGS, JR., ET AL.,

           Plaintiffs

   vs.

R. W. ELLIOTT, Chairman, ET AL.,

           Defendants

ASSIGNMENT OF ERRORS AND PRAYER FOR REVERSAL

    HARRY BRIGGS, etc., and all the others who are plaintiffs in the above-entitled cause, in connection with their appeal to the Supreme Court of the United States, hereby file the following Assignment of Errors upon which they will rely in their prosecution of said appeal from the order and decree of the District Court entered on March 13, 1952:

    1. The District Court erred in refusing to enjoin the enforcement of the laws of South Carolina requiring racial segregation in the public schools of Clarendon County on the ground that these laws violate rights secured under the equal

#1
Im.

The Assignment of Errors and Prayer for Reversal appeal petition in the *Briggs v. Elliott* case, signed by Thurgood Marshall, is shown above. The document outlines the plaintiffs' argument against the original ruling.

Marshall and his fellow LDF attorneys—Spottswood Robinson, Oliver Hill, Jack Greenberg, Robert Carter, and others—knew, in organizing their strategy for presenting their cases to the Supreme Court, that they would have to convince the court to throw out precedents and a host of legal decisions regarding segregation that had taken place during the first half of the twentieth century. They had always hoped for the day when the Supreme Court's 1896 decision, *Plessy v. Ferguson*, would be overturned. They would have to convince the court to cast aside such earlier decisions as *Cumming v. Richmond County Board of Education*, *Berea College v. Kentucky*, and *Gong Lum v. Rice*. In place of these decisions, Marshall and his team would have to push forward the merits of more recent cases—*Gaines v. Canada*, *Murray v. Maryland*, and *Sweatt v. Painter*. If they could do that, perhaps they could convince the Supreme Court that there were no longer any legs—moral, ethical, social, and legal—for *Plessy v. Ferguson* to stand on.

EQUAL·JUSTICE·UNDER·LAW

7

Their Day in Court

After preparing for weeks, Marshall and the NAACP received news from the Supreme Court. The hearings for the *Briggs* and *Brown* cases were to be postponed from their October date to December 8. (The court had decided to delay hearing the cases until after the presidential election.) At that time, the court also informed Marshall and his team that they were going to add the Virginia case, *Davis v. County School Board of Prince Edward County*, to the two other cases. Then, in November, the court agreed to add the two Delaware cases of *Belton* and *Bulah*. In all, the court was ready to hear five cases presented as a legal package in December.

The Supreme Court that Marshall and his colleagues would address was a complicated group of justices. There were serious divisions between its members in the early 1950s. Rarely did the nine justices agree on any issue placed before them. In 1951, the previous year, they only voted unanimously in one out of every five decisions. The court's chief justice, Fred M. Vinson, and four other justices—Harold H. Burton, Stanley F. Reed, Sherman Minton, and Tom C. Clark—generally supported the federal government's interests in cases. They were conservative men on the court, anxious in those days about the spread of communism, both in and outside the United States.

At the other end stood two justices—Hugo L. Black and William O. Douglas. They often thought the power of the federal government was too extensive and they served as watchdogs of the people, intent on protecting the rights and privileges

Chief Justice Fred Vinson (pictured front row, center) heard the initial arguments of the Brown case, but was later replaced by Warren Burger.

of Americans, especially if the threat appeared to come from the government. Wedged in between these two extremes were Justices Felix Frankfurter and Robert H. Jackson. It was their middle-ground view that the court's sole obligation was to simply interpret the law and uphold the Constitution. They were not engaged in the concept of the court using its power to create new laws and change the social order, a practice often referred to today as "legislating from the bench." It was the job of Congress to make national law and the court's job to interpret those laws. Despite the differences in their approaches to the law or their opinions on the power of the government versus the power of the people, however, the nine men on the Supreme Court in the early winter of 1952 knew that the collection of race and education cases that they were scheduled to hear were as controversial as any the court had faced in many years.

With all these cases being approved for a single Supreme Court hearing, the work of the NAACP became more complicated. Fortunately for the court, the LDF had been involved in these cases already and were familiar with them in every way. To complicate things further, though, each case also included lawyers from different areas—from Topeka, Kansas; Clarendon and Prince Edward counties, Virginia; and Delaware.

A separate segregation school case was also scheduled for a hearing, one the NAACP had not participated in. Marshall had passed on the case that became known as *Bolling v. Sharpe* because it involved schools in the District of Columbia that were administered, as mandated by the U.S. Constitution, by the U.S. Congress, not the states. Since he and his colleagues were seeking cases involving segregation by states, the *Bolling* case did not serve the NAACP's purposes. Trying to strike down *Plessy v. Ferguson* required the questioning of the practice of denying citizens their rights as granted under the Fourteenth Amendment to the U.S. Constitution, which barred such denial on the part of the *states*, not the *federal government*. Although *Bolling v. Sharpe* would be heard in December, it was decided separately, not as part of the package of cases to be presented by the NAACP lawyers.

Less than two weeks before Marshall and his team were scheduled to present their case to the Supreme Court, they gathered at the Howard University law school, to engage in a mock trial. Law professors played the roles of the Supreme Court justices and asked difficult questions of the NAACP legal team to help them prepare even further for the historic hearing. The exercise served as a dress rehearsal for the hearing. When it was over, Marshall and the others "felt thoroughly prepared to present the most important case of their lives."[78] Despite their preparations, however, they still felt the pressure of knowing that the future of millions of blacks across America hung in the balance that December.

THE HEARING BEGINS

At 1:35 on the afternoon of December 9, 1952, the hearing began that would give the U.S. Supreme Court the opportunity to decide the future of racial segregation in the United States. As soon as the justices filed into the room and took their seats, LDF attorney Robert Carter took his place at the lectern and presented his arguments regarding the *Brown* case. The NAACP attorneys had decided to use the Constitution's Fourteenth Amendment as the centerpiece of their case. The amendment seemed clear: "No state has any authority under the equal protection clause of the Fourteenth Amendment to use race as a factor in affording educational opportunities among its citizens."[79] Carter argued that Linda Brown had been victimized not by the condition of her schoolhouse, but by the policy of segregation itself. The Fourteenth Amendment was intended to secure the equal rights of all Americans, and Linda Brown and other students in the Topeka school system had been denied a portion of those rights.

Concerning *Plessy v. Ferguson* and its 60-year-old concept of "separate but equal," Carter argued that the landmark nineteenth-century Supreme Court decision was never intended to apply to racial discrimination to public schools. He then cited the Supreme Court's decisions in both *Sweatt* and *McLaurin*. Although these two cases applied to schools of higher learning such as universities and graduate schools, Carter argued that the same logic should be applied to public schools. There should be no role of segregation anywhere in the public schools of America. Of course, even as Carter was stating his case, he appealed to the justices to knock the precedent of *Plessy* off its pedestal. He gave social science data and studies that indicated that segregation "instilled feelings of insecurity and inferiority" in black students.[80] He presented signed affidavits from 35 experts confirming his facts and theories.

Throughout the second half of Carter's presentation, the Supreme Court justices bombarded him with questions, interrupting him frequently. One of the justices, Felix Frankfurter, asked a question that cut directly to Carter's point concerning his view of *Plessy*. After reminding the court that *Plessy* had been a matter of public law for decades and that the courts, including the Supreme Court, had already considered its ramifications repeatedly, Justice Frankfurter asked Carter if he understood that he was asking that "this Court, should now upset so long a course of decisions?"[81] Carter's response was clear and equally to the point: "I have no hesitancy in saying that the issue of 'separate but equal' should be faced... and should be squarely overruled."[82]

Carter's presentation was countered by the lawyer representing the state of Kansas, Paul Wilson, the state's assistant attorney general. Although he did not take much time for his presentation, he stated that previous legal decisions and court precedents had allowed states to "classify citizens by race,"[83] which was certainly the case with segregation laws: "We have never at any time entertained any doubt about the constitutionality of our statute. We think the question before this Court, is simply: Is the Plessy case... and the 'separate but equal' doctrine still the law of the land?"[84] By the time Wilson finished his presentation to the court, he and Carter had taken only 90 minutes of the court's time.

Then, at 3:15 P.M., Thurgood Marshall stood before the justices to present his arguments regarding the *Briggs* case. As Marshall spoke that day, despite the anxious months of preparation that had preceded that afternoon, the veteran lawyer remained collected and even relaxed. When the justices asked him a question, he answered them back in an almost friendly manner so that "Marshall's exchanges with the justices seemed more like a conversation among acquaintances than a historic argument before the nation's highest tribunal."[85] In many ways, Marshall's arguments mirrored those that had just been made by Carter. He decried the segregation practiced in Clarendon County. He believed the system that treated black students so unfairly was unconstitutional, because, according to Marshall, it violated the tenets of the Fourteenth Amendment that guaranteed equality rights under the law. The skilled NAACP lawyer cited previous decisions the Supreme Court had made that had restricted the states from passing laws that the court considered unconstitutional. Marshall, too, cited the conclusions of social scientists and psychologists concerning the damaging effects of segregation on black children.

Just as he had questioned Carter, Justice Frankfurter questioned Marshall concerning what might happen if *Plessy v. Ferguson* was overturned: "I think that nothing would be worse than for this Court . . . to make an abstract declaration that segregation is bad and then have it evaded by tricks."[86] Marshall stated almost matter-of-factly that the court would certainly have the power to counter such steps. If school officials tried to redraw districts to keep black students all in their own schools, the NAACP attorney explained that they could be taken to court again. In an effort to calm the justices concerning how complicated desegregation might prove to be, Marshall assured the court: "It might take six months to do it one place and two months to do it another place."[87] Unfortunately, Marshall's time estimates proved more than optimistic.

The questions would continue coming from Frankfurter:

> Frankfurter continued to pepper Marshal with questions, asking if South Carolina had the right to make any classification based on differences among children. For example, could a state separate smart students from dumb students? What if there was a good reason for having separate schools for blue-eyed children? Would Marshall object to a plan to have "all blue-eyed children . . . go to separate schools"? Decisively, Marshall answered: "No, sir, because the blue-eyed people in the United States never had the badge of slavery which was perpetuated in the [segregation] statutes."[88]

As Marshall's presentation and arguments were similar to Carter's, so Judge Davis's arguments were similar to the Kansas assistant attorney general's. Similarly, just as Marshall had been poised and polished before the justices, so was Davis. He stressed the ways in which South Carolina had already changed its schools to make them more equal between the races, and he placed an emphasis on the accepted rule that states had a right to enact laws based on racial classifications. He argued that the "scientific" evidence that had been presented was under debate and that even if everything the social scientists had said were true, operating separate schools by race in America was legal and that it did not violate the Fourteenth Amendment. The authors of the Fourteenth Amendment had "intended to allow racial segregation."[89] Lastly, Davis emphasized the importance of a state retaining the right to control and regulate the system of schools it operated on behalf of its own children. Local control of schools was always the best policy. In Davis' words:

> Is it not a fact that the very strength and fiber of our federal system, is local self-government in those matters for which local action is competent? Is it not, of all the activities of

government, the one which most nearly approaches the hearts and minds of people, the question of the education of their young?[90]

Following Davis's arguments, Marshall had time before the justices for rebuttal to answer anything Davis had questioned concerning Marshall's earlier presentation before the court. The veteran NAACP lawyer did not let any of Davis's points remain intact. In Davis's questioning of the scientific data, Marshall reminded the court that Davis had not attempted to disagree with the data directly with evidence of his own. Just as he had argued in his initial presentation, Marshall again stated that the segregation practiced by the state of South Carolina had no legal basis under the law.

By the second day of the hearing, Spottswood Robinson appeared before the justices arguing the appeal of *Davis v. County School Board of Prince Edward County*. Since the NAACP lawyers had collaborated and all had the same goals for each of their cases, Robinson's presentation made the same general arguments that had been made by Carter and Marshall. He reminded the court that the Virginia lower court had acknowledged that the black schools were not equal to the white schools in the state but that the court had made a mistake in deciding that the county was responsible for improving the separate black schools to make them more like the white schools. Robinson said the lower court should have ordered desegregation and allowed black students into previously all-white schools. Robinson's legal counterpart was particularly aggressive in his presentation to the court, accusing the NAACP of creating the legal problems in the first place. It was the civil rights group that had caused the strike at Moton High School, attorney Justin Moore claimed. He was highly critical and skeptical of the testimony of Dr. Kenneth Clark, claiming the psychologist "was a man of warped judgments who had spent little time in the South and did not really know its people."[91]

Louis J. Redding (left) confers with Thurgood Marshall at the Supreme Court during a recess. Redding was the first African American attorney in the state of Delaware.

When it came time for the Delaware case to be presented, Albert Young, the state's attorney general, spoke first; he was appealing the lower state court's decision that had been in favor of the NAACP's case. As others before, Young told the court that state and local school officials were already in the process of remedying the inequities in the state's schools and that the lower court's decision to integrate the schools was premature and unnecessary. The LDF attorney, Jack Greenberg, argued that Delaware's improvement plan for its black schools was still ill-formed and vague and that the only acceptable decision was to allow Delaware's schools to become integrated.

For three days, the presentations before the Supreme Court continued on. The District of Columbia's *Bolling v. Sharpe* case was also presented to the justices, but it was not part of the legal canopy jointly referred to as *Brown v. Board of Education*. Then, near 4 P.M. on December 11, the arguments were over, and the cases had all been presented. Marshall and his team, all of whom were exhausted emotionally and physically, left the court building, anxious to leave the city and get home to their families. The Christmas holiday was, after all, just around the corner. They were anxious for the court's decision, but their work was completed, and the court could take as much time as it needed. It never occurred to anyone that the court would take as much time as it would.

A LONG DELAY AND A DEATH

Although Marshall and his colleagues had done a solid job of presenting their arguments and evidence before the Supreme Court, victory was not assured. Even Marshall was concerned how the justices would decide. He believed he and his NAACP colleagues would win three of the five cases, including those in South Carolina, Virginia, and Delaware. He did not think the Kansas case would go their way, since Kansas's facilities for black and white school children were not that different. As for the fifth case, the District of Columbia was federal property and the role of the state in public education was not an issue there.

As the justices of the Supreme Court began to consider their rulings in the cases before them, they knew they had more than one obligation to consider. They had to look at the arguments that had been presented to them directly, as well as earlier court rulings, and render a decision. They knew, too, that their decision would impact the future of segregation in America, for if they ruled it unconstitutional, much of the American school system would be forced to fundamentally change. What kind of timetable should they give to the thousands of school boards that would be required to make the appropriate changes to come in line with such a decision by the court?

Through the opening months of 1953, the justices wrestled with these and other issues surrounding *Brown v. Board of Education of Topeka*. Through those difficult and indecisive weeks, it became clear that Chief Justice Vinson, as well as Justices Reed and Clark were not completely supportive of the NAACP's call for desegregation. Justices Black, Douglas, Burton, and Minton were leaning the other way. Two remained undecided, including Frankfurter and Robert Jackson. Even as late as June, a full six months after the case had been presented, Frankfurter was still undecided. On June 8, he asked that the case be presented again for reargument sometime later in the year. The court was woefully deadlocked.

The announcement came as a shock to Marshall, his team, and the nation in general, but the justices had key concerns and questions they could not get beyond in making their ultimate decision concerning *Brown v. Board of Education*. Each was crucial: "Did the framers of the Fourteenth Amendment intend to end school segregation? Did the Supreme Court have the power to abolish school segregation? And how would school integration be managed if the court voted to mix black and white schoolchildren?"[92] The reargument was scheduled for October but was later moved to December, just as had happened the previous year.

The call for reargument may have had an additional motive, as well. The Republicans had won the presidential election the month before the first presentation of *Brown* to the Supreme Court. The new president, Dwight D. Eisenhower, had just been sworn in in January and his administration, should the court decide in favor of integration, would have to oversee the changes in public schools directly. Some of the justices wanted to know if President Eisenhower would support integration. As a later chief justice of the Supreme Court, Warren Burger, would observe: "They wanted to get them into the act. So they had them reargue it, and then the [new] government was to file a brief as a friend of the court."[93]

Just as they had the previous year, the NAACP team spent much of their summer working through the questions the justices had put to them, especially in search of the historical roots and intentions of those who participated in the passage of the Fourteenth Amendment. The new expert social scientists were historians. Marshall lined up Professor John Hope Franklin, who taught history at Howard University to head the research concerning "how the Fourteenth Amendment had been put in practice after ratification in 1868."[94] He also assigned a white historian, Alfred Kelly, from Wayne University in Detroit, to similar research. The search through the historical records proved disappointing, however, because "most of the research indicated that the congressmen who wrote the Fourteenth Amendment, and state legislators who ratified it, had no intention of integrating schools."[95] Marshall tried to put as positive a spin as he could on what the historians had uncovered.

By the fall, the NAACP lawyers still had lingering questions and doubts of their own concerning the reargument that was looming before them. (At that time, the scheduled date was still in October.) Then, in an event that no one saw coming, the direction of the future decision concerning *Brown v. Board of Education* took a decisive turn. On September 8, at 3:15 A.M., Chief Justice Vinson died suddenly of a heart attack in his Washington apartment. Vinson's death put the scheduled reargument on hold while President Eisenhower made his decision on whom to appoint as the new chief justice. Within weeks, Eisenhower tapped the governor of California, Earl Warren. Warren accepted and was sworn in on October 5. (He immediately became the acting chief justice, although he would not be confirmed by a vote of the Senate until March 1954.) As for the *Brown* reargument, it was postponed until December.

THE FINAL PRESENTATION

The reargument was scheduled to begin at 1 P.M. on December 7, 1953. People began lining up outside the Supreme Court build-

Crowds of people wait in line for the chance to secure one of the 50 seats set aside for the public in the second round of arguments for the *Brown* case.

ing 12 hours earlier, in hopes they could watch the proceedings. When Marshall and his colleagues presented to the newly led Supreme Court, they had changed their previous strategy slightly. With little historical evidence revealing a direct intent to desegregate schools, Marshall decided his team should "focus on the spirit of the discussion surrounding the enactment of the Fourteenth Amendment."[96] In court, he argued that those who had created the Fourteenth Amendment clearly had a goal in mind and that was to erase racial inequality in America. They would attempt that, argued Marshall, by guaranteeing the rights of every American and the equal protection of those same rights by altering the U.S. Constitution.

The reargument opened with a presentation by Spottswood Robinson, who outlined the case that had previously been argued by the NAACP: that the Fourteenth Amendment had been written to defy racial discrimination. Marshall followed Robinson. He argued once more that *Plessy v. Ferguson,* as well as more recent cases such as *Gong Lum v. Rice,* had been decided in error by the Supreme Court nearly 60 years earlier.

Judge Davis was again in the court hearing room as the opposition lawyer, arguing against Marshall and noting seven specific Supreme Court decisions that had upheld *Plessy* and the concept of "separate but equal." It should remain for the states to determine the nature of their own educational system, and Davis told the justices that the Supreme Court "cannot sit as a glorified board of education for the state of South Carolina or any other state."[97]

The following day, the reargument continued, as Marshall returned to the podium to rebut the arguments made by Davis and others the previous day. Marshall noted that the defense attorneys had supported continuing segregation by arguing that it had existed for 90 years since the end of the Civil War; that it was the way things should be and that it was best for both races. The shrewd NAACP lawyer addressed both arguments:

> I got the feeling on hearing the discussion yesterday that when you put a white child in a school with a whole lot of colored children, the child would fall apart or something. Everybody knows that is not true. . . . Those same kids in Virginia and South Carolina—and I have seen them do it— they play in the streets together, they play on their farms together, they go down the road together, they separate to go to school, they come out of school and play ball together. They have to be separated in school.[98]

On the second day of the reargument, Marshall performed brilliantly. (He had some problems the previous day as the justices had "found his arguments weak; they openly showed a lack of interest and left Marshall fumbling before he finally stopped."[99]) Day two was a different story, however. Paul Wilson, the attorney representing Kansas, noted the difference: "This time he took a different, more effective approach—he came on like a locomotive."[100] When Marshall finished his arguments, his work was done a second time on behalf of *Brown v. Board of Education*. Just as with the previous year's hearing, once the presentations were over, it was again in the hands of the nine black-robed justices of the Supreme Court.

Again, months passed without a decision from the court. May arrived, and still no decision. Marshall became concerned that the court might not make a decision until their following term. Mid-May found Marshall in Mobile, Alabama, where he had spoken that Sunday, May 16. He was preparing to take a flight to Los Angeles the following day for another speaking engagement, "when he received a phone call—he never said from whom—telling him that he might want to be at the Supreme Court instead. Marshall caught the next flight to Washington."[101]

A HISTORIC DECISION

All through the months between December 1953 and May 1954, Chief Justice Warren oversaw one of the most important Supreme Court decisions of the twentieth century. When the reargument had ended, most of the members of the court had not had their questions adequately answered by either side. In the days immediately following the reargument, it became clear that the court was not prepared to vote unanimously. Warren did weigh in and stated his belief that "de jure [that enacted into law] segregation was unconstitutional."[102] He told his fellow justices that "the more I've read and heard and thought, the more I've come to conclude that the basis of segregation and 'separate but equal' rests upon the concept of the inherent inferiority of the colored race."[103] In taking this view, Warren was skirting around the issue of what the framers of the Fourteenth Amendment *intended*. Instead, he was taking a moral position.

Although he did not have a unanimous court, with his appointment to the court, he headed a majority of justices who were ready to strike down *Plessy v. Ferguson*—including Douglas, Black, Burton, and Minton. The others remained at various

The Supreme Court justices who decided the *Brown v. Board of Education* case are pictured on May 17, 1954. Chief Justice Earl Warren appears in the front row, center.

positions toward the opposite view. For the next three months, Warren continuing calling his justices together to discuss the case with the intent of them making a decision. He worked continually on Justice Frankfurter, who "was struggling to find a constitutionally satisfactory means of joining Warren and the others."[104] Warren took Reed—perhaps the strongest holdout—to lunch frequently, telling him that desegregation was "the best thing for the country."[105] By the end of March 1954, Warren had seven of his fellow justices ready to strike a blow against *Plessy* and in favor of desegregation. When Reed appeared to be the only holdout, Warren reminded him "that he stood alone and that a dissent would encourage resistance in the South. Did Reed really wish to do that?"[106] Once Warren assured Reed that he would give the South time to make the significant change of desegregation, however, the holdout justice agreed. Warren would have his unanimous decision.

The announcement came at 12:52 P.M. on May 17, 1954. Before a group of reporters gathered in the Supreme Court's press room, Chief Justice Warren began unfolding the court's decision. He took time to go over the facts surrounding the case and how it had come finally before the Supreme Court. He spoke of the intent of the framers of the Fourteenth Amendment. He referred to *Plessy v. Ferguson*. He made it clear, however, that the decision was not simply based on history: "In approaching this problem, we cannot turn the clock back to 1868 when the Amendment was adopted, or even to 1896 when *Plessy v. Ferguson* was written. We must consider public education in the light of its full

WARREN'S JOURNEY TO THE SUPREME COURT

When chosen by President Eisenhower to head the Supreme Court, Earl Warren was instantly a controversial pick. Justice Frankfurter was disappointed that Eisenhower had not selected a notable judge to the leadership position on the court. Frankfurter considered Warren nothing more than a "politician." Americans were pleased with Warren's appointment, however. He had gained his law degree from the University of California and been a public servant for many years, including serving as assistant counsel for the city of Oakland. He subsequently had become district attorney, then attorney general of California.

As governor, he had been progressive, supporting the construction of new highways, hospitals, and schools. He even tried to establish a state health insurance program. Warren also supported anti–lynching legislation and actively sought to remove the poll tax in California. His political aspirations led him to run in 1948 as the vice presidential running mate to Democratic candidate Thomas Dewey. In 1952, he switched parties and sought the Republican nomination for president, losing instead to Eisenhower. In time, Eisenhower would regret his development and present place in American life throughout the Nation."[107] The Chief Justice continued speaking to those waiting to hear the court's decision: "Does segregation of children in public schools solely on the basis of race, even though the physical facilities and other 'tangible' factors may be equal, deprive the children of the minority group of equal education opportunities? We believe that it does."[108] Then, Warren spoke the words that mattered; the words that would rewrite American history:

> We conclude that in the field of public education the doctrine of 'separate but equal' has no place. Separate

choice of Warren for the court, "when Warren led the Court in an activist, liberal direction." Since Eisenhower was conservative on almost every issue, he later told friends privately that appointing Warren was the "biggest damn fool mistake" of his entire career.*

Under Warren's leadership, however, the court gained a new sense of direction and cohesion. Many on the court had not liked Vinson's leadership, and they found Warren "courteous, graceful, a patient, retentive listener, and dignified without being in any way pompous. Within weeks he had managed to establish cordial relations with all his colleagues."** By the time the *Brown* rehearing came before the justices, "the Court was already becoming a more harmonious and purposeful body than it had been for some time."***

* Quoted in James T. Patterson, *Brown v. Board of Education: A Civil Rights Milestone and Its Troubled Legacy.* New York: Oxford University Press, 2001, p. 60.
** Ibid.
*** Ibid.

Attorneys George Hayes (left), Thurgood Marshall (center) and James Nabrit (right) congratulate one another on the steps of the Supreme Court, after the *Brown* decision was announced in 1954.

educational facilities are inherently unequal. Therefore, we hold that the plaintiffs and others similarly situated . . . are . . . deprived of the equal protection of the laws guaranteed by the Fourteenth Amendment.[109]

Sitting in the room, hearing these words spoken by the chief justice of the U.S. Supreme Court, Thurgood Marshall, who was ordinarily on his feet, loud, boisterous, and gregarious, sat in stunned silence. Later, he explained: "I was so happy I was numb."[110] He did not remain silent for long. He turned to the two attorneys who had argued the District of Columbia case, James Nabrit II and George Hayes, and told them both: "We hit the jackpot."[111] Soon afterward, newspaper reporters surrounded Marshall, all in search of a quote from the NAACP's best and brightest. The following morning, Marshall was quoted as saying: "It is the greatest victory we ever had . . . the thing that is gratifying to me is that it was unanimous and on our side."[112]

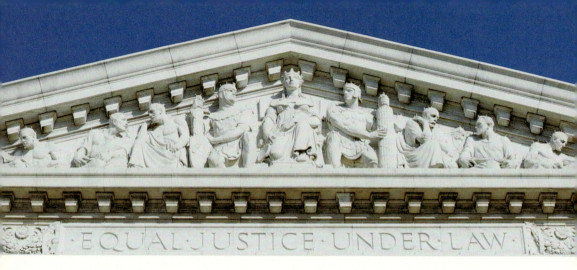

EQUAL JUSTICE UNDER LAW

8

An Endless Road

arren's announcement to the press and to the waiting world concerning the court's decision to strike down *Plessy v. Ferguson* and a near century of segregated schools in America was only 2,000 words long and had taken a matter of minutes to read. The importance of the court's unanimous decision would be staggering, however, one that would require more change than Americans had seen in many decades, perhaps centuries. It was immediately front page news. Newspapers—north, south, east and west—trumpeted the official end to segregation in public schools, but the tone of the headlines varied widely from one geographic region to another.

A *New York Times* editorial stated that the Supreme Court's decision "squared the country's basic law with its conscience and deepest convictions."[113] A writer for the *Chicago Defender*, a black newspaper, compared the decision to the impact of an atomic bomb: "This means the beginning of the end of the dual society in American life."[114] The *Pittsburgh Courier*, another important black newspaper, stated the global effects the *Brown* decision would have: "The conscience of America has spoken through its constitutional voice . . . It will effectively impress upon millions of colored people in Asia and Africa the fact that idealism and social morality can and do prevail in the United States regardless of race, creed, or color."[115] In the Midwest, Iowa's *Des Moines Register* announced that the

On the day following the landmark Supreme Court decision, the *New York Times* printed word of the 9 to 0 vote.

GETTING A CASE TO THE UNITED STATES SUPREME COURT

Since the ratification of the U.S. Constitution in the late 1780s, America's highest court has been the U.S. Supreme Court. The intent of creating such a court was to help provide a balance between the three main branches of the federal government (also created by the U.S. Constitution)—the executive, legislative, and judicial branches. For more than two centuries, the Supreme Court has heard thousands of cases, mostly in the form of appeals, granting the final legal word on issues ranging from the power of the federal government to parental rights. For consistency on the court and to eliminate as much as possible the possibility of outside political influence, justices appointed to the Supreme Court serve for life. They may, however, choose to step down at any time.

Not all lower court cases that are appealed are taken up by the Supreme Court. Today, with all the court cases taking place in the country each year, this would be impossible. The court and its justices hear only the cases they want to hear. The process of getting a case on the docket of the Supreme Court is not exactly a simple one.

In most instances, if lawyers want their cases brought before the U.S. Supreme Court, they must file a document known as a writ of certiorari with the court. The point of this starting document is to move a case from a lower court to the Supreme Court. For a case to be accepted by the court, at least four of its justices (today, the Supreme Court has nine) must agree that the case should receive a hearing. Generally, cases are accepted by the Supreme Court for a hearing when they involve either a constitutional issue or a state court's decision as it effects federal law, or when two courts reach two different rulings in the same case.

When the justices agree to hear a case, it is the responsibility of the case's lawyers to prepare to present their arguments before the court. First, they submit briefs, which comprise their arguments on paper. The briefs include references to legal documents, which also must be included in the briefs, as well as the precedents, if there are any, that relate to the case at hand. Others may also submit briefs relevant to the case. These may be organizations or groups that have a stake in the eventual decision or would be directly impacted. They are called "friend of the court," the legal Latin term being *amicus curiae.*

Once a case has been accepted by the Supreme Court, the justices read the briefs of both sides and file their own briefs concerning the case. The court will schedule oral presentations during which the attorneys representing their clients will present directly to the justices and then field questions put to them by the court. If the court has accepted "friends of the court," they will have an opportunity to present, as well. Once all sides have presented to the court, the justices will have time to confer among themselves, as well as check up on facts presented in court. Then the court decides. Supreme Court decisions are simple majorities, five of nine justices. When an important case is being considered, however, one that would have far reaching results, the court's head, the chief justice, typically encourages as many justices as possible to decide the same way. Ideally, they could make a unanimous decision.

Above all, the justices on the Supreme Court are quite reluctant to overturn the decisions made by an earlier Supreme Court, especially because they often base their opinions on the same decisions that have set precedent for later courts. The Supreme Court, from time to time, comes to view society and the law differently than a previous court. When the court overturns a decision made by its predecessors, it often has a dramatic impact on American society. This was certainly what was at stake when the Supreme Court took up the race cases concerning public schools in the early 1950s.

court "has begun the erasure of one of American democracy's blackest marks."[116]

Many southern newspapers wrote their headlines concerning the Supreme Court's decision with bitter pens, sometimes with threats. The newspaper for the University of Virginia, the *Cavalier Daily*, decried the decision, complaining that it would destroy a way of life that had existed since the early 1600s, one based, of course, on slavery and racism. In Jackson, Mississippi, the *Daily News* made a dire prediction, stating that "blood may stain Southern soil in many places because of this decision."[117] There would be incidents of opposition to the decision before its ink was dry. White supremacist groups across the South gained new members and some new groups were formed, as well, including the White Citizens' Council. This racist organization was established in Mississippi by a white circuit court judge, Tom P. Brady. The group met for the first time two months following the *Brown* decision, and others joined the group from across the South in the months that followed. The council was intent on opposing the *Brown* decision and supporting the conceit that whites were superior to blacks and that the races should be kept separate.

ANOTHER DECISION BY THE COURT: BROWN II

Despite the importance of the Warren court's decision that segregation in America's public schools was unacceptable, it would only be the first step in a process that would require yet another hearing before the court. That May, the justices had only stated that school segregation was against the law; they said nothing about how the schools across the country would tear down their existing systems and make room for integration. That situation required a second decision, one that would come to be known as Brown II. Warren decided to hold the question of how and when until the court's next term. What was needed was for the court to establish a timeframe by which integration would need to take place.

In the aftermath of *Brown*, integration was underway shortly where local school officials decided they were going to abide by the court's decision and not fight it. In many places across the South, the change from separation to integration was done quietly, without incident, as schools opened their doors for black students. Just four months after the initial Warren court decision, a school in the small community of Charleston, Arkansas, became the first school to integrate in the 11 southern states that had made up the Confederacy during the Civil War. Others fell into step and changed southern history:

> During the 1954–1955 school year, students in Washington, D.C., Louisville, Baltimore, and St. Louis began attending

Clinton High School in Knoxville, Tennessee, was the first high school in the South to be integrated after the *Brown* decision. When the town was stirred up and riots ensued, white students were put on escort patrol to protect their new classmates.

racially mixed schools. . . . Junior colleges in Texas and public schools in West Virginia voluntarily accepted both black
and white students. In Topeka, the school board had voted
to change its policy even before the second Supreme Court
hearing.[118]

The Brown family out in Topeka, by the fall of 1955, sent
Linda's younger sister to school for the first time. She entered an
integrated school that had formerly been all-white.

Other schools balked, however. Once again, the NAACP
team was pressed into duty. At the NAACP's headquarters in
New York, Marshall discussed the approach the LDF should take
in the matter with lawyers and experts both in the organization and outside. Spottswood Robinson and Dr. Kenneth Clark
thought the implementation of the court's decision should be
immediate, whereas others advised that the process should be
more gradual, perhaps over a number of years. Marshall and
several other NAACP attorneys decided that desegregation
should not be postponed for long and decided to argue before
the Supreme Court for the process to be completed by 1956.

The hearing for Brown II was scheduled for April 11, 1955,
11 months after Warren's announcement in favor of *Brown*
and against *Plessy*. Arguments stretched over four days and included 13 hours of oral presentation. The following month,
on May 31, Brown II was issued. In making its decision, the
court decided to allow for some compromise. Rather than nail
down a specific timeframe for implementation of *Brown*, the
court announced that integration would have to take place in
America's public schools with "all deliberate speed."[136] The
hope on the part of the justices was that this would especially
give the southern states an opportunity to adjust to the concept and reality of integrating its schools and make the changes in the proper manner and to the proper extent. Also, President Eisenhower had not endorsed the *Brown* decision, and
the Justice Department had made the recommendation that

the nation's school districts would need a significant amount of time for implementation.

This decision by the Supreme Court proved disappointing to Marshall and his colleagues in the NAACP. The southern states took advantage of the Warren court's open-ended time-table and dragged their heels. Two years after the initial *Brown* decision, not a single "black student had been enrolled in a white school in Alabama, Florida, Georgia, Louisiana, Missis-sippi, the Carolinas, or Virginia."[120] Polls taken during the mid-1950s indicated that only one in every five southerners support-ed desegregation. This lack of support for desegregation would lead to confrontations across the South, sometimes even at the schoolhouse door. In the fall of 1957, more than three years

Federal troops escort the "Little Rock Nine" from Central High School in Little Rock, Arkansas, in 1957. The troops were ordered by President Dwight D. Eisenhower to protect the black students from protesting mobs.

Ten years after the *Brown v. Board of Education* decision, Linda Brown, Ethel Louise Belton, Harry Briggs, Jr., and Spottswood Bolling met for a press conference to commemorate the landmark case.

after the initial *Brown* decision, a violent face-off took place at Little Rock's Central High School. With the school scheduled to integrate with the fall term, the state's governor, Orval Faubus, ordered Arkansas National Guard troops to block the door of the school against nine black students who tried to enroll. The confrontation led to a stalemate, until, more than two weeks later, President Eisenhower sent troops from the 101st Airborne Division. On September 25, "one thousand rifle-toting soldiers surrounded the school. Soldiers drove black students to school and walked with them to class."[121] Despite what had been his tepid support of the *Brown* decision before this encounter, Eisenhower was not prepared to allow state officials to stop the implementation of a Supreme Court decision.

The foot-dragging by southern states would continue for several more years. Progress continued, but advancements came slowly and in dribs and drabs. Nearly a decade after the first *Brown* decision, just over half of America's black students were attending racially mixed schools. In some Deep South states, the number was less than 10 percent. Then, in 1964, the Supreme Court made another decision regarding a NAACP school case—*Griffin v. School Board*. The case had originated in Virginia, in the very locale that had been a plaintiff back in the early 1950s—Prince Edward County. The court announced that it would no longer tolerate a postponement by any school concerning integration. One of the justices, Hugo Black, in wording the court's majority decision, announced: "The time for mere 'deliberate speed' has run out and that phrase can no longer justify denying these Prince Edward County schoolchildren their constitutional rights to an education equal to that afforded by the public schools in other parts of Virginia."[122] With another such case four years later, again in Virginia, the court revealed it had lost its patience for delay. The court "ordered school boards to desegregate their schools and eliminate discrimination 'root and branch.'"[123] By then, the black lawyer who had proven so crucial in the long and hard-fought campaign against school segregation had left the NAACP legal team, and for good reason. In 1967, President Lyndon Johnson appointed Thurgood Marshall as a justice on the United States Supreme Court.

Today, integration is the norm in America's public education system. That reality was not accomplished with ease, however, and certainly not overnight. It occurred through the tireless efforts of countless men and women, some white, many black, who took their ideals and dreams about America and what it represents and worked to make them acceptable to the

Thurgood Marshall was appointed to the Supreme Court in 1967. He served the court for 24 years.

vast majority of Americans. For many years stretching from the Civil War and beyond World War II, segregation denied an entire race of citizens in the United States the enjoyment of one of the grandest privileges America has to offer—equal rights for all. Thurgood Marshall and everyone within the NAACP understood segregation's destructive nature, and fought to break a system of racism so the schoolhouse door could be opened to everyone.

Chronology

1600s–1850s	Slavery exists in America; millions of blacks are treated as property.
1861–1865	U.S. Civil War divides the nation between the slave-holding South and the free states of the North.
1863	President Abraham Lincoln issues his Emancipation Proclamation, which frees slaves held in southern states that seceded from the Union.
1865	The Thirteenth Amendment is ratified by the states, bringing slavery in America to a legal end.
1866	The 1866 Civil Rights Act guarantees certain rights to America's blacks and implies that free blacks have U.S. citizenship.
1868	The Fourteenth Amendment is ratified, providing equal rights for blacks.
1870	The last of the three Reconstruction Amendments, the Fifteenth, is ratified by the states granting and guaranteeing blacks the right to vote.
1875	U.S. Congress passes the Civil Rights Act, a law intended to fill in gaps existing the guarantee of the freedoms and rights of blacks
1883	U.S. Supreme Court declares the Civil Rights Act of 1875 unconstitutional.
1880s–1890s	Blacks begin to lose their newly gained freedoms, as southern states create laws that skirt the Reconstruction Amendments to the Constitution.
1881	Tennessee legislature passes one of the first "separate but equal" laws, which restricted blacks from riding "whites only" railroad cars. Other southern states soon follow suit.

1896   U.S. Supreme Court upholds the constitutionality of Louisiana's separate car law, thus validating the concept of "separate but equal." *Plessy v. Ferguson* becomes a landmark race decision that remains in place for more than a half century. Segregation between the races becomes normalized in American society.

1910   The National Association for the Advancement of Colored People (NAACP) is established.

1952   Marshall and other NAACP attorneys appear before the Supreme Court for a hearing of the *Brown v. Board of Education of Topeka* case.

1953   After months of deliberation, the Supreme Court, deadlocked on a decision on the *Brown* case, requests that the case be reargued later that year.

Timeline

1863
Abraham Lincoln issues his Emancipation Proclamation.

1866
The 1866 Civil Rights Act guarantees certain rights to America's blacks.

1875
U.S. Congress passes the Civil Rights Act.

1863 ... Congress shall make no law respecting an ... **1881**

1865
The Thirteenth Amendment is ratified.

1868
The Fourteenth Amendment is ratified.

1870
The the Fifteenth Amendments, is ratified by the states.

1881
Tennessee legislature passes one of the first "separate but equal" laws.

1953 Before the *Brown* case is reargued, the Supreme Court's Chief Justice Vinson dies suddenly of a heart attack.

1953 President Eisenhower appoints Earl Warren as the Supreme Court's new chief justice.

1953 The *Brown* case is reargued before the Warren court.

1954 Marshall wins a landmark decision from the U.S. Supreme Court. The decision, *Brown v. Board of Education of Topeka*, strikes down the concept of "separate but equal" and segregation in the establishment of public schools in the United States.

1955 The Supreme Court hears oral arguments from Marshall and other NAACP lawyers regarding the implementation of the earlier *Brown* decision.

1910
The National Association for the Advancement of Colored People (NAACP) is established.

1952
NAACP attorneys appear before the Supreme Court for *Brown v. Board of Education of Topeka*.

1954
Marshall wins *Brown v. Board of Education of Topeka*, striking down the concept of "separate but equal."

1910 **1964**

1950
Thurgood Marshall wins *Sweatt v. Painter* and *McLaurin v. Oklahoma State Regents for Higher Education*.

1953
Brown is reargued before the Warren court.

1955
The Warren Court issues Brown II.

1964
Supreme Court decides *Griffin v. School Board*, through which the Court stated that its "timetable" for "all deliberate speed" had run out.

1955   The Warren Court issues Brown II, which announces that America's public schools must be integrated with "all deliberate speed."

1967   President Lyndon Johnson appoints Thurgood Marshall to a seat on the U.S. Supreme Court.

Notes

Introduction

1. Quoted in James T. Patterson, *Brown v. Board of Education: A Civil Rights Milestone and Its Troubled Legacy* (New York: Oxford University Press, 2001, p. 52).

2. Quoted in Juan Williams, *Thurgood Marshall: American Revolutionary* (New York: Three Rivers Press, 1998, p. 216).

Chapter 1

3. Quoted in Darlene Clark Hine, *The African-American Odyssey* (Upper Saddle River, NJ: Prentice Hall, 2005, p. 298).

4. Quoted in James Tackach, *Brown v. Board of Education* (San Diego: Lucent Books, 1998, p. 17).

5. Quoted in Harvey Fireside and Sarah Betsy Fuller, *Brown v. Board of Education: Equal School for All* (Hillside, NJ: Enslow Publishers, 1994, p. 23).

6. Quoted in Edward L. Ayers, *The Promise of the New South: Life After Reconstruction* (New York: Oxford University Press, 1993, p. 136).

7. Quoted in William H. Chafe, Raymond Gavins, and Robert Korstad, eds., *Remembering Jim Crow: African-Americans Tell About Life in the Segregated South* (New York: New Press, 2001, p. 72).

8. Quoted in Fireside and Fuller, *Brown v. Board of Education,* p. 23.

9. Quoted in Hine, *The African-American Odyssey,* p. 316.

Chapter 2

10. Quoted in Fireside and Fuller, *Brown v. Board of Education,* p. 25.

11. Quoted in Harvey Fireside, *Separate and Unequal: Homer Plessy and the Supreme Court Decision That Legalized Racism* (New York: Carroll & Graf Publishers, 2004, p. 224).

12. Quoted in Hine, *The African-American Odyssey*, p. 337.
13. Ibid., p. 341.
14. Ibid., p. 370.
15. Ibid., p. 372.
16. Quoted in Tackach, *Brown v. Board of Education,* p. 30
17. Ibid., p. 31.
18. Ibid.

Chapter 3

19. Quoted in Robert J. Cottroll, Raymond T. Diamond, and Leland B. Ware, *Brown v. Board of Education: Caste, Culture, and the Constitution* (Lawrence: University of Kansas Press, 2003, p. 55).
20. Ibid., p. 56.
21. Ibid., p. 57.
22. Ibid., p. 60.
23. Quoted in Williams, *Thurgood Marshall*, p. 96.
24. Ibid., pp. 96–97.
25. Quoted in Fireside and Fuller, *Brown v. Board of Education*, p. 33.
26. Ibid.
27. Quoted in Tackach, *Brown v. Board of Education*, p. 38.

Chapter 4

28. Quoted in Tackach, *Brown v. Board of Education*, p. 39.
29. Ibid.
30. Quoted in Williams, *Thurgood Marshall*, p. 183.
31. Ibid.
32. Ibid.
33. Ibid.
34. Quoted in Tackach, *Brown v. Board of Education*, p. 41.
35. Quoted in Williams, *Thurgood Marshall*, p. 185.
36. Ibid., p. 184.
37. Quoted in Tackach, *Brown v. Board of Education*, p. 41.
38. Ibid.
39. Quoted in Williams, *Thurgood Marshall*, p. 185.

Chapter 5

40. Quoted in Williams, *Thurgood Marshall*, p.195.
41. Ibid., p. 187.
42. Ibid.
43. Quoted in Tackach, *Brown v. Board of Education*, p. 46.
44. Quoted in Williams, *Thurgood Marshall*, p. 201.
45. Quoted in Tackach, *Brown v. Board of Education*, p. 46.
46. Ibid., p. 50.
47. Quoted in Susan Dudley Gold. *Brown v. Board of Education: Separate but Equal?* (New York: Benchmark Books, 2005, p. 48).
48. Ibid., p. 49.
49. Quoted in Cottroll, et al., *Brown v. Board of Education*, p. 128.
50. Ibid.
51. Ibid., p. 130.

52. Quoted in Tackach, *Brown v. Board of Education*, p. 51.
53. Ibid., p. 52.
54. Ibid.
55. Quoted in Cottroll, p. 130.
56. Ibid., p. 132.
57. Quoted in Tackach, *Brown v. Board of Education*, p. 52.
58. Quoted in Gold, *Brown v. Board of Education*, p. 52.

Chapter 6

59. Quoted in Cottroll, et al., *Brown v. Board of Education*, p. 134.
60. Ibid.
61. Quoted in Tackach, *Brown v. Board of Education*, p. 52.
62. Quoted in Cottroll, et al., *Brown v. Board of Education*, p. 134.
63. Quoted in Tackach, *Brown v. Board of Education*, p. 52–53.
64. Ibid., p. 53.
65. Ibid.
66. Quoted in Cottroll, et al., *Brown v. Board of Education*, p. 135.
67. Quoted in Tackach, *Brown v. Board of Education*, p. 55.
68. Quoted in Cottroll, et al., *Brown v. Board of Education*, p. 136.
69. Ibid., p. 137.
70. Ibid.
71. Ibid.
72. Ibid.

73. Quoted in Gold, *Brown v. Board of Education*, p. 55.
74. Quoted in Williams, *Thurgood Marshall*, p. 209.
75. Ibid., p. 210.
76. Ibid., pp. 210–211.
77. Ibid, p. 210.

Chapter 7

78. Quoted in Tackach, *Brown v. Board of Education*, p. 59.
79. Quoted in Gold, *Brown v. Board of Education*, p. 58.
80. Ibid.
81. Quoted in Tackach, *Brown v. Board of Education*, p. 61.
82. Ibid.
83. Ibid.
84. Quoted in Gold, *Brown v. Board of Education*, p. 59.
85. Quoted in Cottroll, et al., *Brown v. Board of Education*, p. 140.
86. Quoted in Gold, *Brown v. Board of Education*, p. 61.
87. Ibid.
88. Quoted in Williams, *Thurgood Marshall*, p. 217.
89. Quoted in Cottroll, et al., *Brown v. Board of Education*, p. 141.
90. Quoted in Gold, *Brown v. Board of Education*, p. 62.
91. Quoted in Tackach, *Brown v. Board of Education*, p. 62.
92. Quoted in Williams, *Thurgood Marshall*, p. 219.
93. Ibid., p. 220.
94. Ibid.
95. Ibid., p. 221.

96. Quoted in Tackach, *Brown v. Board of Education*, p. 67.
97. Ibid., p. 70.
98. Ibid., p. 71.
99. Quoted in Williams, *Thurgood Marshall*, p. 223.
100. Ibid., p. 224.
101. Ibid., p. 225.
102. Quoted in Patterson, *Brown v. Board of Education*, p. 64.
103. Ibid.
104. Ibid.
105. Ibid.
106. Ibid., p. 65.
107. Quoted in Tackach, *Brown v. Board of Education*, p. 73.
108. Ibid.
109. Ibid., p. 74.
110. Quoted in Williams, *Thurgood Marshall*, p. 226.
111. Ibid.
112. Ibid., p. 227.

Chapter 8

113. Quoted in Tackach, *Brown v. Board of Education*, p. 75.
114. Quoted in Gold, *Brown v. Board of Education*, p. 81.
115. Quoted in Cottroll, et al., *Brown v. Board of Education*, p. 185.
116. Quoted in Tackach, *Brown v. Board of Education*, p. 75.
117. Quoted in Gold, *Brown v. Board of Education*, p. 82.
118. Ibid., p. 85.
119. Quoted in Cottroll, et al., *Brown v. Board of Education*, p. 185.
120. Quoted in Gold, *Brown v. Board of Education*, p. 93.
121. Ibid., p. 98.
122. Ibid., p. 108.
123. Ibid.

Glossary

affidavit   A sworn statement in writing.

abolitionist   Person who worked to end slavery.

appeal   To have a higher court review a decision made by a lower court.

contempt   Showing disobedience or disrespect to a court or judge.

dissent   A differing opinion.

integrate   To open a place to members of all races and ethnic groups.

mandate   A formal order or command from a superior court.

plaintiff   A person who brings about legal action.

precedent   A court decision that establishes an example for similar cases in the future.

segregation   The separation of people of different races, genders, or other social groups.

statute   An act passed by a legislative body.

Bibliography

Ayers, Edward L. *The Promise of the New South: Life After Reconstruction*. New York: Oxford University Press, 1993.

Boyd, Herb. *We Shall Overcome*. Naperville, Ill.: Sourcebooks Media-Fusion, 2004.

Chafe, William H., Raymond Gavins, and Robert Korstad, eds., *Remembering Jim Crow: African-Americans Tell About Life in the Segregated South*. New York: New Press, 2001.

Cottroll, Robert J., Raymond T. Diamond, and Leland B. Ware, et al. *Brown v. Board of Education: Caste, Culture, and the Constitution*. Lawrence: University of Kansas Press, 2003.

D'Souza, Dinesh. *The End of Racism: Principles for a Multiracial Society*. New York: The Free Press, 1995.

Fireside, Harvey, and Sarah Betsy Fuller. *Brown v. Board of Education: Equal School for All*. Hillside, N.J.: Enslow, 1994.

———. *Separate and Unequal: Homer Plessy and the Supreme Court Decision That Legalized Racism.* New York: Carroll & Graf, 2004.

Gold, Susan Dudley. *Brown v. Board of Education: Separate But Equal?* New York: Benchmark Books, 2005.

Hale, Grace Elizabeth. *Making Whiteness: The Culture of Segregation in the South, 1890–1940*. New York: Pantheon Books, 1998.

Hine, Darlene Clark. *The African-American Odyssey*. Upper Saddle River, N.J.: Prentice Hall, 2005.

Kraft, Betsy Harvey. *Sensational Trials of the 20th Century*. New York: Scholastic Press, 1998.

Martin, Waldo E., ed. *Brown v. Board of Education: A Brief History With Documents*. Boston: Bedford/St. Martin's, 1998.

Patterson, James T. *Brown v. Board of Education: A Civil Rights Milestone and Its Troubled Legacy*. New York: Oxford University Press, 2001.

Sarat, Austin, ed. *Race, Law, and Culture: Reflections on Brown v. Board of Education*. New York: Oxford University Press, 1997.

Speer, Hugh W. *The Case of the Century: A Historical and Social Perspective on Brown v. Board of Education of Topeka With Present and Future Implications*. Kansas City: University of Missouri, 1968.

Tackach, James. *Brown v. Board of Education*. San Diego: Lucent Books, 1998.

Tushnet, Mark V., ed. *Thurgood Marshall: His Speeches, Writings, Arguments, Opinions, and Reminiscences*. Chicago: Lawrence Hill Books, 2001.

Wexler, Sanford. *The Civil Rights Movement: An Eyewitness History*. New York: Facts on File, 1993.

Williams, Juan. *Eyes on the Prize: America's Civil Rights Years, 1954–1965*. New York: Penguin Books, 1987.

———. *Thurgood Marshall: American Revolutionary*. New York: Three Rivers Press, 1998.

Woodward, C. Vann. *The Strange Career of Jim Crow*. New York: Oxford University Press, 1957.

Further Reading

Books

Aldred, Lisa. *Thurgood Marshall: Supreme Court Justice.* Philadelphia: Chelsea House, 2005.

Anderson, Wayne. *Brown v. Board of Education: The Case Against School Segregation.* New York: Rosen, 2004.

Herda, D. J. *Thurgood Marshall: Civil Rights Champion.* Springfield, N.J.: Enslow, 1995.

Horn, Geoffrey M. *Thurgood Marshall.* Milwaukee: World Almanac Library, 2004.

Patrick, John J. *The Young Oxford Companion to the Supreme Court of the United States.* New York: Oxford University Press, 1994.

Pierce, Alan. *Brown v. Board of Education.* Edina, Minn.: ABDO Publishing, 2005.

Vernell, Marjorie. *Leaders of Black Civil Rights.* San Diego: Lucent Books, 2000.

Web sites

www.civilrights.org/campaigns/brown/

www.cr.nps.gov/nr/travel/civilrights/ka1.htm

www.digisys.net/users/hootie/brown/view.htm

www.landmarkcases.org/brown/home.html

www.nationalcenter.org/brown.html

www.pbs.org/jefferson/enlight/brown.htm

www.watson.ort/~lisa/blackhistory/early-civilrights/brown.html

Picture Credits

Index

About the Author

Tim McNeese is an associate professor of history at York College, in York, Nebraska, where he is in his fifteenth year of college instruction. Professor McNeese earned his associate of arts degree from York College, a bachelor of arts in history and political science from Harding University, and a master of arts in history from Southwest Missouri State University. A prolific author of books for elementary, middle, and high school, and college readers, McNeese has published more than 75 books and educational materials over the past 20 years on everything from Mississippi steamboats to Marco Polo. His writing has earned him a citation in the library reference work, *Something About the Author*. In 2005, he published the textbook *Political Revolutions of the 18th, 19th, and 20th Centuries*. Professor McNeese served as a consulting historian for the History Channel program, "Risk Takers, History Makers." His wife, Beverly, is an assistant professor of English at York College, and they have two children, Noah and Summer, and two grandchildren, Ethan and Adrianna. Readers are encouraged to contact Professor McNeese at tdmcneese@york.edu.